T0302069

# Excellence Beyond Compliance

# Excellence Beyond Compliance

## Establishing a Medical Device Quality System

By
William I. White

CRC Press
Taylor & Francis Group
Boca Raton London New York

CRC Press is an imprint of the
Taylor & Francis Group, an **informa** business

A PRODUCTIVITY PRESS BOOK

Routledge
Taylor & Francis Group
711 Third Avenue, New York, NY 10017

© 2018 by William I. White
Productivity Press is an imprint of Taylor & Francis Group, an Informa business

No claim to original U.S. Government works

Printed on acid-free paper

International Standard Book Number-13: 978-1-138-49147-2 (Hardback)
International Standard Book Number-13: 978-1-351-03258-2 (eBook)

**Library of Congress Cataloging–in–Publication Data**

Names: White, William I., author.
Title: Excellence beyond compliance : establishing a medical device quality system / William I. White.
Description: Boca Raton : Taylor & Francis, 2018. | Includes bibliographical references and index. |
Identifiers: LCCN 2018002607 (print) | LCCN 2018010579 (ebook) | ISBN 9781351032582 (eBook) | ISBN 9781138491472 (hardback : alk. paper)
Subjects: LCSH: Medical instruments and apparatus–Standards. | Medical instruments and apparatus–Quality control.
Classification: LCC R856.6 (ebook) | LCC R856.6 .W45 2018 (print) | DDC 610.28–dc23
LC record available at https://lccn.loc.gov/2018002607

**Visit the Taylor & Francis Web site at**
http://www.taylorandfrancis.com

**and the Productivity Press site at**
http://www.ProductivityPress.com

*To Evelyn Ampofoa,*

*my inspiration for more than 50 years*

# Contents

# Preface

## A COMPLIANCE STORY

About 1100 years ago in what is now northern France, the Viking leader known as Rollo to the Franks ("Rolf" to the Vikings) improved upon a century-old Viking tradition by not only raiding, but occupying Rouen and surrounding territory. The century-old Frankish tradition of persuading Viking leaders to leave by paying large amounts of gold and silver had resulted in a reduced treasury. Hence, the king of the Franks, known as Charles the Simple,[1] determined upon another strategy. The king agreed to acknowledge Rollo's right to a large territory in return for assisting the king to defend against other Vikings. Rollo would also be brought into the family by marrying Charles's daughter Gisela. This was formalized by the treaty of Saint-Claire-sur-Epte in 912.

There were two conditions of compliance for Rollo. First, Rollo had to agree to be baptized; it would not be suitable for a non-Christian to hold such a key position. For whatever reason, baptism turned out not to be an issue. However, the second requirement was more problematic. Feudal custom at the time required Rollo, as a new vassal of his lord, Charles, to kiss Charles's foot. Rollo was not prepared to do this: "I will never bow my knees at the knees of any man, and no man's foot will I kiss." Instead, he delegated the task to one of his men. This man took hold of the king's foot and lifted it to his lips, throwing the king on his back in the process. According to the chronicler this provoked "a great laugh [among the Vikings?] and a great outcry [among the Franks?]."[2]

According to the reports, Rollo went on to become an effective vassal of the king, responsible for a substantial reduction in Viking raids in subsequent years. It appears that Rollo's unorthodox approach to compliance did not in any way detract from his commitment to fulfill his part of the agreement.

---

[1] Unfortunately for Charles, this translation of "Carolex Simplex" has turned out to be more memorable—and thus more frequently used—than the intended meaning of Charles the Straightforward. He was not stupid.

[2] Dudo of St. Quentin, *History of the Normans*, trans. and ed. Eric Christiansen (Woodbridge: Boydell, 1998) as reported in Robert Ferguson, *The Vikings*, London: Penguin, 2009, pp 177–192.

We can learn from this story.

The world of medical device regulations and standards does not normally provide the opportunity for drama along the lines of the story (for which we may be grateful). Nevertheless, these regulations and standards do present almost daily challenges for us to ensure that our companies are compliant. In our efforts, we need to keep in mind that there are a lot of different ways to comply. As quality/regulatory professionals we must find the best ways for our companies.

We need to be as creative as Vikings in our approach to compliance. If compliance is the only goal for our quality management system, we miss a significant opportunity.

- Some attempts at compliance lead to entangling employees in a morass of procedures that seems to have no end. In such cases, where apparently compliance is the only goal, we may not even achieve that goal. Well-meaning but confused employees can do harm to the company, customers, or even patients.
- Other approaches to compliance require such extensive resources that the profitability of the company is threatened. This in turn can lead to inappropriate cost-cutting measures that cause new areas of noncompliance.

On the other hand, compliance achieved through an effective and efficient quality management system can benefit a business, make it more productive, and even create a competitive advantage.

Charting paths for best practices in effective, efficient compliance is the goal of this book.

# About the Author

**William I. White** started Quality System Strategies LLC in 2006, when he retired after 30 years at Bayer HealthCare LLC. At Bayer, after 20 years in R&D, he worked with colleagues in the mid-1990s to establish the design control system for the diagnostics division. He then became manager, Quality Systems Strategy, and in that role served as principal architect for the worldwide quality system of the division.

Since retiring from Bayer, he has advised medical device companies ranging in size from a few persons to several thousand persons on how best to fulfill requirements of 21 CFR 820 and ISO 13485 while creating quality systems that serve the needs of the companies and their employees.

Dr. White holds an A.B. in chemistry from Harvard College and a PhD in chemistry from Cornell University.

# Acknowledgments

I must acknowledge the roles that many people have played in making this book possible.

Foremost is the thanks I owe to Javad Seyedzadeh for inspiring me with a vision of what it is possible to achieve with a quality management system.

For twenty years I have been discussing QMS issues with David Fox, and it seems that every time I talk with him I learn something new. I am much indebted to him also for reading and critiquing in detail the first draft of this book. Daniel Olivier has also inspired me for decades with his practical approach to fulfillment of requirements for quality. Kathleen Roberts has been a source of insight; she also provided useful comments about the first draft of the book. I had the opportunity of working closely for many years with Friedrich Rieger, and owe to him much of my understanding of customer feedback management and Corrective/Preventive Action (CAPA). Marta Chase encouraged me to start consulting; it was truly a pleasure working with her to improve the quality management systems of three different companies. Nadia Hammad gave me the opportunity to explore in detail the subject of design control; she was also my inspiration for continual use of the phrase "Quality is everyone's business." James Monticello provided his unique, ever-positive perspective on the quirky features of more than one quality management system. Nancy Singer's website is a creative source of valuable information about quality and regulatory compliance. Kelly White gave me very useful legal advice.

There are many more persons to whom I am indebted for countless discussions on quality management system features. Some of these are Kofi Akuoko, Margaret Aquila, Dale Beer, Jens Bettin, Sheila Brennen, Paul Brooks, Pamela Burdette-Miller, Thomas Carlson, Fredrick Clerie, Brian Cullinan, Pascal Dwane, Ronda Elliott, Kenneth Emancipator, Wilson Ford, Ian Gavigan, Glen Gershon, Pedro Gonzalez, Bruce Goode, David Gronostajski, John Harris, David Harrison, Barbara Immel, Paul Kehr, Gerd Krisam, Frank LaDuca, Richard Levinson, Betty Loomis, Lynette Makowski, Susan Mecca, Daniel Meyaard, Nancy Miller, Marsha Moore, Renee Nasser, Andreas Neuberg, Kevin Painter, Yves Perradin, Marla

Phillips, Lawrence Picciano, Jon Riddell, Regina Rohe, Linda Salek, Rosanne Savol, Robert Schaeper, Jon Speer, Stephen Stanley, Evan St. Germain, George Tancos, William Tisel, and Carol Walker. In daring to name these, I am sure I have neglected others, whose names I will remember only after this book is in print. I beg their forgiveness.

# Introduction

Many companies limp along from day-to-day treating the quality side of the business as a necessary evil, and doing only what is minimally necessary for compliance to regulations. This kind of approach to compliance almost always results in inefficiencies and sometimes can result in a curious kind of noncompliance. Documentation created with compliance as the sole consideration often ends up confusing the employees who must use the documentation.

This book looks beyond what is necessary for compliance alone to address what makes a quality management system (QMS) both effective and efficient. This book also never forgets that real people must make any QMS work; the book provides a blueprint for creating a QMS that real people will find useful.

After a review of the challenges that any medical device company faces in the world of today—the multiple sources of QMS requirements—the book poses a question: are we satisfied with the QMS we have now, or could we do better? If we want to do better, this book can help.

Chapter 2 suggests a path to follow: first get support from top management, then create a steering committee, and proceed along a defined path.

Chapter 3 identifies a couple of key decisions that must be made by senior management. First, what is the desired level of control? This will not be a concern for a small company at a single site, but it is a vital concern for larger companies. Second, what should be the guiding factor in choosing a structure for the QMS? A structure based on the international ISO 13485 model, one based on an FDA model, or one based on a homegrown model?

A quality plan must then be drawn up to implement a QMS consistent with those decisions. This plan, treated in Chapter 4, must address in realistic terms the human resources necessary, the documentation transitioning, as well as the long-term plans for the software infrastructure. Finally, the plan must be approved at a high enough level so that everyone in the company can feel their management is committed to the project.

Chapters 5 through 9 address documentation to ensure compliance with regulations and standards. Although a QMS is much more than the documentation alone, if the documentation is defective, there will surely be problems. Chapter 5 covers documentation in general: appropriate levels, formats, and cautions. It also addresses the subject of electronic documents and the process necessary to be sure that all requirements are included.

Chapter 6 provides advice for Level 1 documentation (the Quality Policy and the Quality Manual) in terms of both content and how the content is presented. These are documents that go a long way to set the tone for the company's approach to quality and to help each employee see how she or he fits in the company's quality structure.

Chapter 7 addresses Level 2 documentation, and is supported heavily by examples in Appendix C. This is the level that should cover in general terms (but in more detail than what is in the Quality Manual) what needs to be done and the department(s) responsible. Fewer than three dozen procedures should be necessary to address all QMS requirements. Appendix C covers QMS requirements in a total of 20 example procedures. Most employees will need to be familiar with only a few Level 2 procedures.

The details of "how to do what must be done" are identified in Level 3 procedures and is covered in Chapter 8. For multisite companies, this chapter discusses subject areas that should be candidates for multisite Level 3 procedures to ensure uniform handling of issues. The chapter also discusses the structure of Level 3 procedures, supported by examples in Appendices D and E.

Level 4 documentation, covered in Chapter 9, is often a catch-all level. It may include such varied documentation as records, forms, guidance documents, training materials, and external documentation. All are dealt with.

Chapter 10 treats the very important topic of how to incorporate product risk management into the whole of the QMS, not just in product development. The concepts for risk management should be included in the quality manual, throughout the Level 2 documentation, and Level 3 procedures should detail how this must be done.

Implementation is the subject for Chapter 11. Essential for implementation is a realistic assessment of resources necessary, both human and infrastructure. Key concepts for implementation are communication and training. All these subjects are touched on in this chapter.

Chapter 12 handles the very necessary steps for ongoing care and feeding of the QMS. It presents ideas on how to ensure that the QMS undergoes continual improvement. Critical components for maintenance and improvement (that can best be managed by way of a quality council) are metrics, internal audits, and (most important of all) effective management reviews. This chapter also discusses working with Registrars/Notified Bodies. It also addresses developments to watch for the future.

Finally, there are a number of Appendices that will be useful in various circumstances.

Appendix A deals with Pharmaceutical Quality System Models. This may be useful in constructing a QMS for a pharmaceutical manufacturer that also produces medical devices. It will also prove useful for a manufacturer producing a combination product, such as a drug using a device for delivery.

Appendix B addresses the effort on behalf of the International Organization for Standardization to facilitate multiple management systems for the same company. Unfortunately, for reasons explained in the text, the outcome of this ISO effort in the short run is likely to make it more difficult for a medical device company to harmonize with other management systems. However, if a medical device company already has certification to ISO 9001 and wants to maintain that certification, this appendix will facilitate the effort.

Appendix C contains a wealth of information concerning the content of Level 2 procedures. Although in no way claiming to capture all the information needed for a complete QMS, these example procedures address the concepts involved and covers those concepts in detail.

Appendices D and E deal with an important subject, customer feedback management, and provide examples of two different ways to specify how employees need to address the issues arising.

We should close with a cautionary note. This book aims to help with the construction of a QMS, but it is not intended as a substitute for the quality standards and regulations. You will need to purchase a copy of ISO 13485:2016 as well as the current version of ISO 14971—and possibly other standards as well. You will need to read not only 21 CFR 820, but the Preamble to it, and all the other applicable regulations from the United States and around the world that apply to your QMS.

# 1

## *The Challenge*

### OBJECTIVE: GOOD PRODUCTS

Medical device companies seek to place good products in markets around the world in order to provide sound healthcare for patients. They know this means that products—whatever other appealing features they have—should meet certain basic requirements, such as:

a. They should be designed and manufactured to perform as intended taking account of the state of the art.
b. They should be manufactured under an established product risk management system.
c. They should conform to safety principles and risks associated should be reduced.
d. They should be designed for safety of use in the environment where they will be used.
e. They should not compromise health or safety of patients or users when used and maintained as intended throughout the lifetimes of the products.
f. They should not be adversely affected by transportation and storage.
g. They should be stable throughout their intended use life.
h. Risks should be acceptable compared with benefits during normal use.

These are abbreviated versions of the most general of the "Essential Principles of Safety and Performance of Medical Devices and IVD Medical Devices"[1] proposed by the International Medical Device Regulators

---

[1] IMDRF Good Regulatory Review Practices Working Group, "Essential Principles of Safety and Performance of Medical Devices and IVD Medical Devices," GRRP WG (PD1) N47. The final document will be available some time after April 2018 through the International Medical Device Regulators Forum, http://www.imdrf.org.

Forum (IMDRF).[2] The best medical device companies ensure that such principles are incorporated into the way they do business.

One of the ways they achieve this is by establishing an efficient and effective quality management system (QMS). A good QMS facilitates implementation of these essential principles. It also provides a foundation for compliance with medical device regulatory requirements in all the markets where the company sells its products.

## COMPLIANCE IS FUNDAMENTAL

Compliance with medical device regulations is essential. A company out of compliance faces the possibility of a cascade of ever-increasing negative consequences.

Findings of a U.S. Food and Drug Administration (FDA) investigator at an inspection are listed on Form 483. If the findings are sufficiently serious, they can lead to a Warning Letter. A Warning Letter alone can have adverse financial implications for the company:

- Federal agencies are advised of Warning Letters so that they can take this into account in awarding contracts.
- Premarket approvals may be held up until the violations have been corrected.
- Requests for Certificates for Foreign Governments (needed to place a product on the market in some countries) will not be granted until the violations that may be related to those products have been corrected.
- Manufacturers outside the United States receiving an FDA Warning Letter face the prospect of import refusal in what may be their largest market.

When the FDA perceives that a Warning Letter has not led to adequate improvement, they may take actions that have even higher costs, such as

---

[2] The International Medical Device Regulators Forum (IMDRF) has been established as a joint effort by governments to promote harmonization of medical device regulations around the world. Their documents are worthy of diligent study.

regulatory fines, consent decrees, and civil or criminal actions. Such actions by the FDA can make a company more vulnerable to liabilities in lawsuits.

Although regulatory actions by the FDA are often of highest concern to a company, other regulatory authorities around the world can have a major impact on profitability for a company. In general, these authorities seek to work with companies to resolve compliance problems short of major regulatory action. Nevertheless, if they perceive it necessary, they can take significant steps, the first of which is normally refusal to allow importation.

Ultimately the biggest downside to compliance issues made public through regulatory actions can be the loss of customers simply from harm to a company's reputation in the marketplace.

## THE MOVING TARGET

Always difficult, the task of building compliance into a QMS has become continually more complex.

- In the 1990s European Medical Device Directives[3] obliged medical device companies to heed the requirements of quality standards that evolved into the stand-alone quality system standard, ISO 13485:2003.[4]
- In 1997 the FDA implemented the most critical quality system requirements as the Quality System Regulation.[5] FDA requirements related to quality systems go beyond these basic requirements, and include, among others, regulations for adverse events[6] and recalls.[7]
- The international standard ISO 13485:2003 provided a reasonable basis for international harmonization in intervening years. However, as each new country has adopted this standard as a foundation for its approach, each has found appropriate reasons for adding to these

---

[3] 90/385/EEC, Active Implantable Medical Devices Directive, 93/42/EEC, Medical Devices Directive, and 98/79/EC, *In Vitro* Diagnostic Medical Devices Directive.

[4] International Standard, ISO 13485:2003, Medical devices—Quality management systems—Requirements for regulatory purposes.

[5] FDA, 21 CFR 820, Quality System Regulation.

[6] FDA, 21 CFR 803, Medical Device Reporting.

[7] FDA, 21 CFR 806, Medical Device Corrections & Removals.

provisions or modifying them. Examples are: Canada,[8] China,[9] Brazil,[10] Australia,[11] Japan,[12] and Tanzania.[13]

- Moreover, some European countries expressed concerns that the 2003 standard did not cover requirements of the medical device directives in sufficient detail to justify its designation as a harmonized standard. This led to the creation of BS EN ISO 13485:2012, a standard that duplicates the text of the 2003 standard but contains in addition three annexes that detail the relationship between paragraphs of the directives and clauses of the standard.[14]

- In the meantime, efforts were ongoing to update the 2003 standard more fully, in accordance with the normal practice for standards managed by the International Organization for Standardization (ISO). Although a transition period is allowed during which the 2003 standard continues to be acceptable, quality management systems now being designed or revised should be based on the new standard, ISO 13485:2016.[15] A very helpful guide to the transition from the 2003 to the 2016 version has been published by ISO.[16]

In addition to these challenges, there are further complicating factors:

- The international product risk management standard ISO 14971:2007,[17] although nowhere formally required, has become an essential document in assuring safe and effective medical devices

---

[8] Medical Devices Regulations SOR/92-282 (promulgated 1998).

[9] Medical Device Good Manufacturing Practice, China Food and Drug Administration, December 2014.

[10] RDC 16, 28 March 2013, GMP Certification and Maintenance for Medical and In Vitro Devices; RDC 15, 28 March 2014, Requirements related to proof of compliance with Brazil GMP, ANVISA (Agência Nacional de Vigilância Sanitária).

[11] Australian regulatory guidelines for medical devices, Version 1.1, May 2011, Therapeutic Goods Administration.

[12] Japanese Ministry of Health, Labor and Welfare (MHLW) Ordinance No. 169, Ministerial Ordinance on Standards for Manufacturing Control and Quality Control for Medical Devices and In Vitro Diagnostic Reagents, MHLW, December 2004.

[13] Guidelines on Submission of Documentation for Registration of Medical Devices, Tanzania Food and Drugs Authority, 2nd edition, October 2016.

[14] BS EN ISO 13485:2012, Medical Devices—Quality management systems—Requirements for regulatory purposes.

[15] BS EN ISO 13485:2016, Medical Devices—Quality management systems—Requirements for regulatory purposes. This revision also includes annexes detailing the relationship between paragraphs of the European directives and clauses of the standard.

[16] ISO 13485:2016—Medical devices—A practical guide, 2017. This guide provides valuable general advice for quality-management systems to meet the requirements of the standard.

[17] International Standard, ISO 14971:2007, Medical devices—Application of risk management to medical devices.

worldwide. The incorporation of its requirements into the quality management system of each medical device company is essential to success. This situation is further complicated through issuance of ISO 14971:2012[18] as a harmonized standard for Europe with annexes addressing the particular requirements of European medical device directives.

- An increasing number of products are combination products— usually a device together with a therapeutic agent. Although the regulatory approaches for such products are evolving around the world (and thus not yet completely clear), there is usually an expectation that the quality management system (QMS)/good manufacturing practices (GMP) regulations for both components must be met. This provides additional challenges for any QMS.

- There are many advocates of the concept that companies can be most effective and efficient when they combine management systems, such as: quality, environment, safety, and finance.[19,20] Although it is not clear that any medical device companies have chosen to go down this path, the approach is likely to be of value to those that do.

- A further complication is a recently published framework for all future revisions to management system standards that has as a goal to make it easier for companies to adopt multiple standards in this manner.[21] Ironically, for medical device companies this new framework is likely to have the opposite effect, since the structure of ISO 13485:2016 is the same as the 2003 version, rather than the new framework preferred by ISO.

Despite challenges posed by moving targets, there is no barrier to a company that wants to establish a QMS that meets all requirements in an efficient and effective manner. The first step is the identification of those requirements.

---

[18] BS EN ISO 14971:2012, Medical devices—Application of risk management to medical devices (ISO 14971:2007, Corrected version 2007-10-01).

[19] International Organization for Standardization, The integrated use of management system standards, 2008.

[20] Sandford Liebesman, *Competitive Advantage: Linked Management Systems*, Chico, CA: Paton Press LLC, 2011.

[21] International Organization for Standardization, Annex SL, Proposals for management system standards.

## WORLDWIDE REQUIREMENTS

### United States

Any medical device company located in the United States (as well as any company that wishes to sell in the United States) will have as a primary focus the applicable FDA regulations, some of which have explicit implication for the QMS, and others of which need to be included at some level within the QMS.

- 21 CFR 820, Quality System Regulation. In addition, the Preamble[22] provides important insight on interpretation.
- 21 CFR 803, Medical Device Reporting.
- 21 CFR 806, Medical Devices: Reports of Corrections and Removals, which should be addressed in conjunction with 21 CFR 7, Enforcement Policy.
- 21 CFR 821, Medical Device Tracking Requirements in the event that the company has products that require tracking.

Although these four regulations are the only ones likely to be addressed in routine inspections, each company must ensure that it fulfills requirements of all applicable regulations. Additional examples that should be addressed by company documentation where applicable include:

- 21 CFR 11, Electronic Records; Electronic Signatures
- 21 CFR 801, Labeling
- 21 CFR 807, Establishment Registration and Device Listing for Manufacturers and Initial Importers of Devices
- 21 CFR 809, In Vitro Diagnostic Products for Human Use
- Multiple regulations for addressing clinical trials, including: 21 CFR 812, Investigational Device Exemptions; 21 CFR 50, Protection of Human Subjects; 21 CFR 54, Financial Disclosure by Clinical Investigators; and 21 CFR 56, Institutional Review Boards
- 21 CFR 822, Postmarket Surveillance

In the event that a medical device company is manufacturing a combination product (drug and/or biologic plus a device) the applicable regulation is 21 CFR 4, Regulation of Combination Products.

---

[22] Federal Register: October 7, 1996 (Volume 61, Number 195), pp. 52601–52654.

In addition to regulations, the FDA has issued many guidance documents. Although most guidance documents express FDA views related to specific categories of products, there are also guidance documents on various aspects of quality management systems. Some examples are:

- Design Control Guidance for Medical Device Manufacturers, March 11, 1997
- General Principles of Software Validation; Final Guidance for Industry and FDA Staff, January 11, 2002
- Quality System Information for Certain Premarket Application Reviews; Guidance for Industry and FDA Staff, February 3, 2003
- Distinguishing Medical Device Recalls from Medical Device Enhancements/Guidance for Industry and Food and Drug Administration Staff, October 15, 2014

Moreover, there may be QMS implications in guidance documents that appear to be product-specific. The FDA issued a guidance in 2012 entitled "Factors to Consider When Making Benefit-Risk Determinations in Medical Device Premarket Approval and *De Novo* Classifications." This document in many ways by implication provides updated guidance on FDA expectations for design control.[23] It is prudent to review guidance documents as they are issued to determine which aspects of those documents should be incorporated explicitly into company procedures.

## Canada

Canadian QMS requirements are summarized in Canadian Medical Devices Regulations, SOR/98-282, the current version of which is available on the Health Canada website (https://www.canada.ca/en/health-canada.html). Canadian regulations are based on ISO 13485, but in addition, there are a number of Canadian-specific requirements. These Canadian-specific requirements are logical concerns of a governmental agency attentive to the health and well-being of its citizens. They include assurances that:

- Only products approved for Canada can be shipped to Canada.
- Canadian complaints are addressed in an appropriate manner.
- Adverse events related to Canada are reported as specified.

---

[23] William I. White, Benefit-risk determinations in design control, *Medical Device and Diagnostic Industry*, February 2012, 28–31.

- Clinical trials conducted in Canada meet specified requirements.
- Information about the manufacturer on the ISO 13485 certificate, the product licenses, and the labeling is consistent.

The Guidance Document GD210, "ISO 13485:2003 Quality Management System Audits Performed by Health Canada Recognized Registrars" is an excellent source enumerating the additional quality system components required for Canada beyond the standard quality requirements. It is available through the Health Canada website.[24] It would be very helpful to manufacturers if other countries basing their device regulations on ISO 13485 would follow this example as a succinct summary of national QMS requirements going beyond that QMS standard.

## Europe

The current framework for medical device regulation in Europe is complex. In 2017 it consists of three directives:

- Directive 90/385/EEC, Active Implantable Medical Devices
- Directive 93/42/EEC, Medical Devices
- Directive 98/79/EC, In Vitro Diagnostic Medical Devices

These have been supplemented by modifying directives, with the last technical revision being Directive 2007/47/EC. A significant number of guidance documents are available through the European Commission website (https://ec.europa.eu). Many of these guidance documents include recommendations that companies can incorporate into procedures.

The regulatory framework in Europe is in process of change from directives that must be implemented separately by each country to regulations intended to ensure uniformity throughout Europe. Two regulations have been established:

- Medical Device Regulation (incorporating requirements for active implantable medical devices)[25]
- IVD Regulation[26]

---

[24] GD210 may be updated for ISO 13485:2016. However, Health Canada may instead rely on the documentation for the MDSAP program. See Chapters 5 and 12.

[25] Regulation (EU) 2017/745 of the European Parliament and of the Council of 5 April 2017 on medical devices.

[26] Regulation (EU) 2017/746 of the European Parliament and of the Council of 5 April 2017 on *in vitro* diagnostic medical devices.

These regulations establish significant new challenges for manufacturers.

The regulations are more prescriptive than the directives. However, if companies have already incorporated the expectations of the published European guidance documents into their quality management systems, they will find that they have already implemented many—perhaps most—of the new requirements.

Nevertheless, there are several aspects of these regulations that require companies to address new issues.

- There is a requirement that each company must have a "qualified person" responsible for regulatory compliance.
- There are substantial new requirements for product approval.
- There are new requirements for clinical evaluations.

Latest date for compliance to the Medical Device Regulation is May 2020, and the latest date for compliance to the IVD Regulation is May 2022. As usual in such cases, companies that plan early for implementation of these changes will be at an advantage.[27]

To fulfill European requirements it has long made sense for a company to obtain certification to ISO 13485 as a starting point. It is technically correct that neither the current medical device directives nor the planned medical device regulations require a company to be certified to ISO 13485. For years, however, companies have realized that it is much more straightforward to be certified compliant to that standard than to be audited separately for all the QMS requirements of the directives/regulations. The recently issued BS EN ISO 13485:2016 is a fully recognized harmonized standard for Europe, with Annexes ZA, ZB and ZC clarifying the relationship of the standard to the directives. It is expected that these annexes will be updated for the medical device regulations. Companies planning to sell product in Europe will find their simplest path almost certainly involves certification to the requirements of ISO 13485.

The departure of the United Kingdom from the European Union is not likely to have a significant effect on QMS requirements for a medical device company. Whatever the details of the regulatory approach chosen

---

[27] Early planning is certainly advisable but may not even be sufficient. In addition to the new requirements for manufacturers, there are new requirements for Notified Bodies, and some Notified Bodies are reducing the scope of their operations, leaving some of their clients out in the cold. During the transition, this will surely produce pain for many manufacturers. A valuable source of information on the new European regulations and their implications has been the Blog of Erik Vollebregt: https://medicaldeviceslegal.com.

by UK authorities, that approach will surely be based on ISO 13485, and is likely to resemble strongly the new European regulations. Developments should be monitored and plans made accordingly, but the UK departure should be no cause for concern related to a manufacturer's QMS. However, the UK exit may cause difficulties with regard to product registration.[28]

## Latin America

The countries of Mercado Común del Sur (MERCOSUR)—Argentina, Brazil, Paraguay, Uruguay, Venezuela, and Bolivia—have specified expectations of a quality system resembling a combination of the requirements of both 21 CFR 820 and ISO 13485:2003.[29] MERCOSUR documents require national implementation by each country, and to date Brazil has been the most enterprising in pursuing quality system approval prior to product approval, at least for higher-risk products.[30]

Requirements for Mexico are identified in a guidance available through the Comisión Federal para la Protección contra Riesgos Sanitarios (COFEPRIS), the Federal Commission for the Protection against Sanitary Risk, an organ of the Department of Health.[31] The requirement is for a certificate of Good Manufacturing Practice from the health authority of the country of origin or a CE mark, an ISO 13485 certificate or a Certificate of Free Sale that includes the GMP assurance.

## Asia

Working Group 3 of the Asian Harmonization Working Party (AHWP, which includes countries outside of Asia)[32] is promoting harmonization

---

[28] Notice to Stakeholders, "Withdrawal of the United Kingdom and EU rules in the field of industrial products," 22 January 2018, European Commission, Brussels, Belgium.

[29] MERCOSUR/GMC/Res. No. 20/11, Reglamento Técnico MERCOSUR de buenas practices de fabricación de productos medicos y productos para diagnóstico de uso in vitro. Although generally consistent with these two documents, the MERCOSUR document places stronger emphasis on risk management and control of consultants. In addition, there is a requirement not only that the Design Output be approved by signature and date, but that the Design History File be approved in the same manner.

[30] Brazilian resolution RDC 16/2013, March 28, 2013; Brazilian resolution RDC 15/2014, March 28, 2014; Brazilian resolution RDC 179/2017, September 27, 2017. Brazil is also a participant in the FDA's Medical Device Single Audit Program (MDSAP) program; see Chapter 5.

[31] Lineamientos para obtener el registro sanitario de un dispositivo médico asi como la autorización para la modificación a las condiciones de registro. http://www.cofepris.gob.mx/AS/Documents/RegistroSanitarioMedicamentos/req_dm.pdf.

[32] Membership includes countries from the Middle East, Africa, and South America, as well as Asia: Abu Dhabi, Bahrain, Brunei, Cambodia, Chile, China, Taiwan (Chinese Taipei), Hong Kong, India, Indonesia, Jordan, Kenya, Korea, Kuwait, Laos, Malaysia, Mongolia, Myanmar, Pakistan, Philippines, Saudi Arabia, Singapore, South Africa, Tanzania, Thailand, Vietnam, Yemen and Zimbabwe.

of quality system requirements to ISO 13485. Member states of ASEAN (Association of Southeast Asian Nations)[33] have agreed to an ASEAN Medical Device Directive.[34] Nevertheless, regulatory requirements remain fundamentally at the country level. Particularly important are:

- In China, State Council Decree No. 680, "Supervision and Regulation of Medical Devices," May 19, 2017, includes a requirement for ISO 13485 certification, Establishment Registration from the FDA for U.S. companies, or Manufacturing License for Japanese or Korean companies. In December 2017, the CFDA published a Draft for Comments version of the Drug and Medical Device Overseas Inspection Regulations, including the possibility of unannounced audits. The working language for the audits will be Mandarin.[35]
- In India, Medical Device Rules, 2017 were released in January 2017, and takes effect as of January 1, 2018. These rules have QMS requirements essentially the same as ISO 13485.[36]

In Japan, MHLW Ministerial Ordinance No. 169, 2004, specifies a quality system that is similar to ISO 13485, but is not identical. Japan is a participant in the MDSAP program (see Chapters 5 and 12). (Japan is not a member of the AHWP or ASEAN.)

## Australia

The Australian approach to medical device regulation is quite similar to the European model but is not identical.[37] As for Canada, a quality system fulfilling requirements of ISO 13485 is necessary but not sufficient to meet Australian requirements. The referenced guidelines, as well as other guidelines available on the Therapeutic Goods Administration website (www.tga.gov.au), address the additional requirements and generally provide useful information for manufacturers.

---

[33] Brunei, Cambodia, Indonesia, Laos, Malaysia, Myanmar, Philippines, Singapore, Thailand, and Vietnam.

[34] ASEAN Medical Device Directive, ASEAN Secretariat, Jakarta, Indonesia, 2015.

[35] This leads to hopes that China might participate in the Medical Device Single Audit Program (MDSAP). See Chapters 5 and 12.

[36] Indian Ministry of Health and Family Welfare, Medical Devices Rules, 2017, New Delhi, January 31, 2017.

[37] Australian Therapeutic Goods Administration, Department of Health and Ageing, Australian regulatory guidelines for medical devices, Version 1.1, May 2011 and What a manufacturer needs to know about conformity assessment and declarations of conformity for IVDs, Version 1.0, November 2011.

### Middle East and Africa

As indicated above, harmonization efforts of several Middle Eastern countries are focused on the Asian Harmonization Working Party.

Many countries in this area expect documentary evidence of product approval in the United States, Europe, or Japan, with some including as options approvals from Canada and/or Australia. Some require also documentary evidence of certification to ISO 13485.

Because of limited resources, some countries in sub-Saharan Africa have very little in place for regulation of medical devices—an unfortunate situation that has potential for exploitation. The World Health Organization (WHO) is promoting a medical device regulatory model that describes a prioritized stepwise approach for countries with limited resources.[38]

---

## MORE REQUIREMENTS

### Product Approval/Registration

Each country or region normally has additional requirements—going beyond quality system requirements—for approval to market medical devices. These are the product-specific requirements aimed at ensuring safe and effective products. It is normally not practical to have quality system procedures for each jurisdiction that address marketing approval, and therefore there is no attempt in this book to cover in detail the regulatory requirements for product approvals. However, each company must have in place a process that ensures fulfillment of marketing approval requirements for each country in which the company intends to sell products. Normally, this is achieved through a well-trained internal Regulatory Affairs staff, augmented, when needed, by external resources.

### Internal Requirements

Any large company may well already have established corporate documents that specify what is required of its sites or divisions in terms of quality and regulatory practices. A site or division establishing its own

---

[38] WHO global model regulatory framework for medical devices including in vitro diagnostic medical devices, Geneva: World Health Organization, 2017.

QMS must be cognizant of these corporate documents and ensure QMS consistency with them.

## Exceptions

Some products in some jurisdictions are exempt from some quality system requirements, such as:

- The FDA exempts most Class 1 products from design control requirements.[39]
- European device directives provide options for product approval that involve external testing of products instead of full examination of the quality system.

Companies should resist the temptation to create quality management systems containing a variety of exceptions.

- Design control represents a common-sense approach to product development that companies should implement for their own benefit, aside from any regulatory requirement.
- It makes no sense for a company to have products approved for Europe through external testing when other jurisdictions require QMS certification.

A standardized approach applied to all products avoids problems arising from confusion as to whether such and such an exception applies.

---

## BEYOND REQUIREMENTS

### Employee Perspective

Employees want to do the right thing—to give customers products that make their lives better and to meet regulatory requirements. It is an unfortunate truth that the QMS itself may provide barriers between the employee who wants to do the right thing and the ultimate goal of effective compliance.

---

[39] 21 CFR 820.1(a)(1) and 21 CFR 820.30(a)(2).

Ironically, one of the most common sources of barriers is excessive zeal in compliance. Sometimes this happens through a succession of external (or even internal) audits. Each audit may identify nonconformities. The nonconformities may lead to new procedures, but don't always lead to revision or elimination of the old procedures, and then procedures are in place that may be inconsistent. Some companies make it easier to create new procedures than to revise old procedures; this phenomenon leads readily to a profusion of inconsistent requirements.

It can also happen that a company finds itself with serious compliance problems and brings in experts to ensure that it has procedures covering all aspects of compliance. In this situation the primary motivation of the experts (understandably) is to ensure that compliance issues are fully addressed in the resulting procedures. If the company is not a full partner in preparing these procedures and simply accepts blindly what the experts are dictating, the result can be procedures so complex that they confuse employees more than they help them.

In short, if not managed well, the complexity that is to some degree required by worldwide regulatory requirements can lead to confusion among employees who are typically struggling to do their best with a workload that can at times feel overwhelming. The QMS must be designed in a manner that helps each employee to do the job effectively and efficiently. This takes some creativity because the target is moving.

## Quality and Regulatory Perspective

As noted above, quality management systems are increasingly required by regulations in countries around the world. This can lead to some confusion related to use of the terms "quality" and "regulatory." In many, perhaps most, companies the Regulatory Affairs department is responsible for obtaining product approvals, whereas the Quality Assurance department is responsible for general oversight of the QMS. In this book the term "regulatory" refers to the legal requirements specified by countries; these may be quality system requirements or product approval requirements. The term "quality" is used to speak of the structures and processes that a company establishes to meet those requirements.

There is a risk that the increasing complexity of regulatory requirements around the world will distract from the opportunity to make the QMS a critical functioning asset for the business. Despite the ever-increasing challenges, with appropriate creativity we can establish quality management systems that align requirements coming from multiple sources and translate these requirements into language that is comprehensible to everyone in the company—not just the quality and regulatory staff. We can do this by focusing first on what is right for customers and patients, and then including any additional regulatory and business-related requirements. The result will be:

- Employees who really understand not just what they are doing, but why they are doing it.
- Employees who are therefore more completely involved in the business.
- Increased business efficiency.
- Competitive advantage in the marketplace.

# 2

## *The Path*

A quality management system (QMS) is a system of processes—processes that are best mapped with flowcharts. The improvement of our QMS is also best managed as a process, for which we can chart the path with a flowchart. Figure 2.1 provides a flowchart-like representation of the steps to follow. In this chapter we discuss this process in general terms. Later chapters address in more detail specific items on the figure.

## ARE WE SATISFIED?

The first step is a decision: Are we satisfied with the QMS we have now?

In formulating our answer to this question, we may want to consider answers to some other questions.

- Do employees have a clear vision of the company's goals for quality and their roles in achieving those goals?
- Have we set our sights high enough? Have we aimed beyond basic compliance?
- Is the QMS seen as an asset to the business?

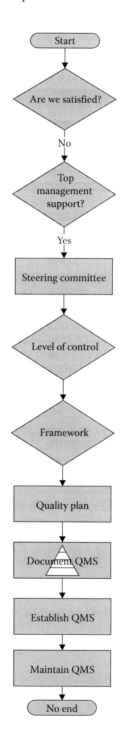

**FIGURE 2.1**
Pathway to a better QMS.

## TOP MANAGEMENT SUPPORT?

How does top management answer this last question? A survey in 2014 found that a substantial percentage of senior executives sees the quality/regulatory function as:

- A necessary evil
- A policeman who says no
- A deterrent to the company reaching its revenue goals[1]

If this is the attitude we find in our top management, the situation presents both a concern and an opportunity. It is a concern because it suggests that we, the quality/regulatory organization, have created a QMS focused only on compliance. It is an opportunity because if we have created the situation, we can change it for the better. We can change the attitude by establishing a better QMS—one in which employees have a clear vision of the company's goals for quality and of their roles in achieving those goals.

If we believe we can do better, one of our first steps must be obtaining the support of senior management. We must convince senior managers that the right approach to quality and regulatory issues can be a source of competitive advantage rather than a barrier to revenue. This can be done by presenting facts in terms of the cost of poor quality, as well as a vision of what an effective and efficient QMS can mean for the business. Business leaders are accustomed to dealing with many risks to the business, and an improved QMS can be presented as a systematic way for them to oversee and reduce the quality and regulatory risks for the business.

It may be possible to establish an effective QMS without the initial support of senior management. One can imagine middle-management beginning by taking a few important steps, showing the benefits and thereby bringing senior management on board.

Nevertheless, the initial struggles to build or rebuild the QMS can be handled so much more easily with senior management support that it is usually worthwhile to spend the time and effort to get that support. If the head of quality is firmly convinced of the value that an effective QMS brings to the business, that person can often convince the president and others on the president's team that the effort is worthwhile.

---

[1] Nancy Singer, Survey Results. https://blog.spartasystems.com/feed/cooperation-regulatory-compliance.

A company is fortunate if its senior management acts to create an effective and efficient QMS without pressure from external forces. Unfortunately, multiple recalls and/or a Warning Letter and its consequences are sometimes needed to convey the message.

## STEERING COMMITTEE

Whatever the motivation of senior management—whether negative such as a Warning Letter or positive such as a desire to implement a better QMS for competitive advantage—a steering committee should be set up to oversee the process. Although leadership of the steering committee should be from the quality/regulatory organization, some members of the committee should be from other parts of the organization. If the effort is perceived as something the quality or regulatory organization is imposing on the company, it is less likely to succeed.

At the start of the process, there are key decisions to be made. The steering committee should consider the options on those decisions and present recommendations to senior management. After those decisions have been made, the steering committee should oversee the creation of a quality plan to implement the decisions.

In the absence of a steering committee, it may be possible for the quality/ regulatory organization to address the key decisions and present recommendations to senior management regarding those decisions. However, by the time of the creation of the quality plan, which will involve essentially all parts of the company, a steering committee or quality council should be established.

## KEY DECISIONS

There are two key decisions that need to be made early in the process of designing the new QMS.

The first is the extent of central control and standardization. For a small company located at a single site this is not really a question: The system established will necessarily be centralized. For larger companies, particularly multinational companies, this is a challenging decision, one that is closely related to the company culture. In some large companies, there is a culture that encourages a high level of local independence; such companies may choose to permit each site to establish its own QMS. Although this is an appealing approach philosophically, it can also add to compliance headaches and infrastructure expenses that would not occur with a more centralized approach.

The second decision needed is to choose a structure for the QMS. Although there is a wide variety of options available, this usually comes down to a question whether to create a QMS with a framework based on a U.S. Food and Drug Administration (FDA) model or a framework based on the process model of the international quality standard ISO 13485. The FDA model was defined to systemize the FDA auditing approach for the Quality System Regulation and divides the QMS into seven subsystems or processes: Management, Design Controls, Corrective and Preventive Action, Production and Process Controls, Equipment and Facility Controls, Records and Documentation, and Material Controls. The ISO model defines four process categories that can be summarized: Management, Resources, Product Realization, Feedback and Oversight. However, the ISO model also requires each company to define its own processes. These can be defined as the same seven subsystems specified in the FDA model; more often, companies choose to define a longer list of processes.

These decisions are discussed in more detail in Chapter 3.

## ESTABLISHING THE IMPROVEMENTS

After these decisions are made, a quality plan must be created and approved by senior management to ensure that all in the company are working toward the same goal—to establish the desired QMS. This plan will state objectives, the steps needed to reach those objectives, and the resources required. The plan is discussed in Chapter 4.

Establishing the improvements begins with documentation—the subject of most of the rest of this book. Although the QMS is a lot more than the documentation alone, good documentation is critical. Good documentation is not sufficient for a good quality system, but it is definitely necessary for one. This subject should be tackled in the order of the levels of documentation:

1. Level 1: Quality Policy and Quality Manual
2. Level 2: High-level procedures stating basic principles and the departments responsible for executing those principles
3. Level 3: Detailed procedures spelling out step by step how the principles are to be carried out

As the documents are created and approved, they must be implemented. Hard copies must be distributed and electronic documents must be made available to those who will use them. Training is essential, with the extent of training proportional to the extent of change. When implementing procedures, a key factor is often the available IT infrastructure. If new software is to be a component of the improvement plan, then the installation of the software requires validation. Throughout the implementation there must be good communication with all in the organization. This ensures early feedback to identify weaknesses that may not have been anticipated, and allows corrective actions needed to fix those weaknesses.

## MAINTENANCE

Maintenance and the question we began with (Are we satisfied?) theoretically should be together at the close of the flowchart. If we ever felt satisfied, of course we could stop. However, even if we had in our company the most effective and efficient QMS we could imagine (a high improbability), regulations may change, interpretations of regulations may change, and quality standards may change. Most of the maintenance can be carried out as corrective or preventive actions under the supervision of the quality council. Some will be significant enough to require a new quality plan. Very serious issues may require rethinking some of the decisions at the top of the flowchart. Even after the original quality plan has been fully implemented, it is best to think of QMS maintenance as a never-ending process.

Through internal quality audits, as well as feedback from customers and other quality data being collected, opportunities for improvement will be identified. Top management will have an opportunity to see this information distilled at management review meetings and can direct needed future improvements.

# 3

## Key Decisions

### LEVEL OF CONTROL

As noted earlier, before a quality plan can be adopted and the work started, senior management need to make some key decisions. Quality and regulatory staff should make sufficient preparations so that they can participate actively in these decisions. Initial decisions include:

- How should company size affect the QMS structure?
- How should company culture affect the approach?
- Do we want one QMS or several?

These questions are all part of the basic question: How much centralized control is appropriate? For small companies at a single location, the QMS approach is straightforward: A single QMS governing the business at that location. However, for larger companies occupying multiple locations—even multiple countries—there are a number of options related to the level of control desired.

As a shorthand for describing the structure options we can use the documentation structure, while at the same time we acknowledge that a QMS is much more than the documentation.

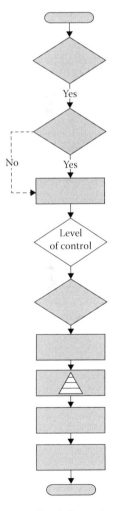

Level of control

23

## Small Company: Straightforward Documentation Structure

A small company at a single site should normally choose a documentation structure consistent with the classical pyramid structure as indicated in Figure 3.1.[1]

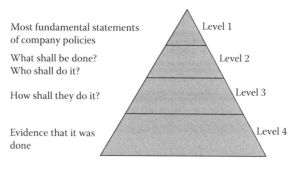

Most fundamental statements of company policies — Level 1

What shall be done? Who shall do it? — Level 2

How shall they do it? — Level 3

Evidence that it was done — Level 4

**FIGURE 3.1**
Classical documentation pyramid.

## Large Company: Several Options

1. Corporate Guidelines

   A large corporate organization guided by a philosophy of complete decentralization and autonomy of each of its sites (or divisions) may choose simply to establish a number of corporate guidelines. Each site is allowed to establish its own QMS to suit local needs, the only proviso being that it must be established in a manner consistent with the principles in established corporate guidelines (Figure 3.2).

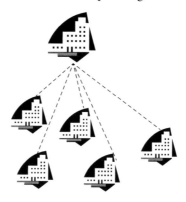

**FIGURE 3.2**
Corporate principles.

---

[1] See Chapter 5 for a more complete discussion of documentation.

2. Corporate Quality Policy and Manual

A corporate organization interested in a somewhat higher level of central control may determine a need for a corporate quality policy and a corporate quality manual to put a corporate stamp on the highest level of QMS documentation. This approach then assumes that each site will establish its own additional levels of documentation consistent with the QMS principles and the documentation structure established in the manual. In this approach it may be appropriate also for each site to have a site-specific addendum to the manual to address exclusions and questions of applicability. For example, some sites may have no design control or complaint call center, or there may be no sterile products at a site (Figure 3.3).

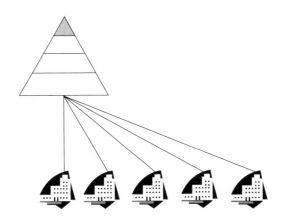

**FIGURE 3.3**
Corporate quality policy and manual.

3. Corporate Manual and Level 2 Documentation

A higher level of central control can be accomplished by adding to the manual a corporate second layer of documentation. Level 2 documentation goes beyond the manual to put in place a more detailed identification of the principles and strategies for the QMS: what must be done (the requirements) and who must do it (the departments responsible for fulfilling the requirements). Sites are then free to spell out in detail how the requirements are to be met, step-by-step (Figure 3.4).

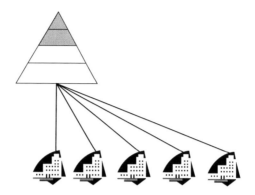

**FIGURE 3.4**
Corporate manual and Level 2.

4. Corporate Manual, Level 2, and Partial Level 3 Documentation
   A wide variety of practical reasons normally dictates that sites must have many processes defined in detail at the site level. Nevertheless, some large companies identify certain key processes that need to be carried out in a consistent manner in detail across all sites. This often happens associated with the establishment of corporate IT systems in which all sites of the company are using a common software application and thus gain particular benefit from a common Level 3 ("how-to") procedure. These companies establish Level 3 work instructions for these key processes in addition to the quality manual and the Level 2 documentation. This represents the highest practical level of central control (Figure 3.5).

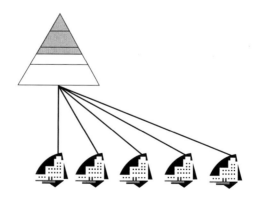

**FIGURE 3.5**
Corporate manual, Levels 2 and 3.

## A Single QMS?

In determining the desired level of control, an important consideration is whether the company intends to have a single QMS across all sites or intends to have each site establish its own separate QMS. This is (or should be) a vital question for any company operating at more than one site.[2]

A single QMS across all sites can benefit a company in many ways.

- It leads to standardization of processes across the organization. Standardization in turn leads to better fulfillment of requirements because there is only one process that all can learn and carry out. It also leads to lower costs from reduced duplication of effort.
- In particular, it leads to lower IT infrastructure costs both in the original installation and validation of QMS software and in the ongoing change control and maintenance.
- Standardization also allows more effective use and sharing of resources.
- It leads to more straightforward interactions with external authorities because complexities of variations at multiple independent sites do not arise. In turn, external authorities can have a high degree of confidence that audit findings at one site can be easily shared across the organization. (In the case of multiple independent sites a significant risk is that information communicated at one site by a regulatory authority may not be adequately shared with other sites.)
- It is easier to ensure compliance because limited resources can be focused on standardized approaches for addressing requirements, rather than having to ensure that requirements are being addressed adequately at multiple independent locations by multiple means.
- It leads to simplified and reduced documentation, which in turn makes compliance more straightforward.
- It helps business operations around the world both to be more involved and to feel more involved in ensuring quality for customers.
- It can help promote the image of the company to the world. For example, a publicly available quality manual for the business posted on a website can serve to emphasize to customers the importance of quality within the company.

---

[2] A secondary question is the decision whether or not to make the incremental additional effort to achieve a single QMS certificate for all of the sites in the QMS. This has the added value of making the registrar a partner in the effort.

In addition to the benefits for the company, a single QMS brings benefits to employees and even customers.

- Quality is everyone's business, and every employee wants to do the right thing. However, complexity and confusion over what to do can make this difficult to achieve. The simplicity of a single QMS can make doing the right thing (compliance) easier.
- When all are able to see their roles within the QMS as a whole, they can do their jobs more effectively.
- When employees do their jobs more effectively, customers and patients benefit as well.

Although there are many benefits to a single QMS for any company, it must be acknowledged that there are at times countervailing forces that may persuade companies to keep separate quality management systems at different sites. For example, if products are completely different from one site to another (sterile vs. nonsterile, Class 2 vs. Class 3, in vitro diagnostics [IVDs] vs. medical devices) there may be a case for keeping separate quality systems. However, historical reasons are rarely adequate to justify maintaining separate quality management systems.[3]

## Choosing Among the Options

On what basis should we choose an option?

Option 1: As noted above, if the corporate culture and philosophy dictate very strongly that central control should be at an absolute minimum and sites (or divisions) should be completely independent, the first option is the most logical. This approach may also be the correct approach if each site is devoted to a substantially different type of product or each site is in a different country with a different primary language.

Options 2, 3, and 4: The other three options are all aimed at achieving a single QMS. They differ in the extent of control exercised by the central organization.

Consideration of the benefits from a single QMS indicates that for most companies, Option 4, with the highest level of central control, will bring the greatest benefits. Standardization of key processes across the whole

---

[3] It is unfortunately the case that some companies operate a curious mixture of quality management systems, with some sites combined into a QMS and other sites combined in slightly different quality management systems. This situation can easily arise through the acquisition process if the company has not fully planned for a comprehensive approach to its QMS.

organization at the level of work instructions provides the most straight-forward route to effective and efficient compliance.

At the same time, even if a company makes this option the ultimate goal, it may be useful to move toward this goal in steps. A company beginning to work by way of guidelines or principles as in Option 1 may choose a gradual path of moving through Options 2, 3, and 4 over a period of years according to an established quality plan.

## FRAMEWORK

After deciding on the appropriate level of control, answers to the next set of related questions will dictate the framework for the QMS.

- Do we want a framework unique to our company?
- Do we want a U.S.-based framework or an international framework?
- How should intended markets for the products affect the decision?
- Should the mix of products affect the framework?

For medical device companies there are multiple choices for structuring the QMS.

- Customized: It would be possible for each company to create a QMS individually that fits the structure of that company.
- FDA models: In guidance documents, the Food and Drug Administration (FDA) has provided approaches for organizing a QMS. In 1999 the FDA published a guidance that organized the Quality System Regulation for medical device companies into subsystems. And in 2006, the FDA published a similar document based on the drug Good Management Practices (GMP) regulations; this might be a choice for a drug company that is also marketing medical devices.

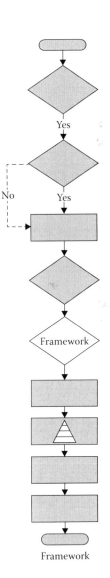

- International models: With the publication of ISO 9001:2000,[4] followed soon after by ISO 13485:2003, the international community has chosen to follow a process-oriented approach.

## Customized Framework

There is nothing sacred about structures arising from FDA or international sources; any structure that provides all required elements can be made successful.

In particular, for a small company at a single location, it may be useful to create a tailor-made QMS, structured to match the company's organization. Reasons for choosing a tailor-made structure may be:

- To have a QMS that is uniquely suited for the company
- To emphasize to employees that the QMS is intended to support the company
- To allow all in the organization to feel a part of something that is unique and special

On the other hand, there may be disadvantages in going down this path.

- In the event of reorganization (always a possibility every few years), the company is faced with a difficult choice: restructure the QMS accordingly or leave the QMS with a structure that may be perceived as out of date.
- New employees coming from another company are likely to be familiar with an FDA or ISO structure and will have a longer learning curve to grasp a special structure.
- External auditors may need extra time or explanation to understand how the QMS components are being addressed.
- The company will need to be particularly vigilant to ensure that all requirements are met.

In the end, it seems likely that for most companies, the disadvantages of a customized structure are likely to be greater than the advantages. This

---

[4] ANSI/ISO/ASQ Q9001-2000, "Quality management systems—Requirements." Note that this is not the current version. A revision was issued as ANSI/ISO/ASQ Q9001—2008, "Quality management systems—Requirements." The current version is ISO 9001:2015; see Appendix B for details.

means that the choice really is between an FDA structure and an ISO structure.

## FDA CGMP Framework

As noted above, in September 2006, the FDA issued a guidance document that describes a quality system approach for drug Current Good Management Practices (CGMP) regulations (21 CFR 210 and 211).[5] This was largely superseded three years later with the publication of a guidance developed by the International Conference on Harmonization.[6] For a medical device division of a larger pharmaceutical organization, this guidance may point toward a logical framework. Appendix A shows in detail the frameworks arising from this guidance and shows the detail of how medical device regulations can fit within a pharmaceutical framework.

## FDA QSIT Framework

For most medical device companies choosing an FDA framework, the framework specifically designed for device regulations is probably the better choice.

Soon after implementation of 21 CFR 820, the FDA determined a need to recast the elements of the regulation in a manner that would facilitate examination during inspections.[7] This "restructuring" is shown in Figure 3.6 and has become commonly known as the QSIT structure (Quality System Inspection Technique).

A company choosing to use a QMS structure based on the FDA QSIT structure will need to add an additional subsystem related to marketing and sales. (Although the Quality System Regulation has no provisions related to sales, there are laws and regulations governing marketing and sales practices that companies must heed and that should be addressed in a complete QMS.) The resulting structure will thus have eight subsystems.

1. Management Controls
2. Design Controls
3. Production and Process Controls

---

5 FDA, "Guidance for Industry: Quality Systems Approach to Pharmaceutical CGMP Regulations," September 2006.
6 FDA, "Guidance for Industry: Q10 Pharmaceutical Quality System," April 2009.
7 FDA, "Guide To Inspections of Quality Systems," August 1999.

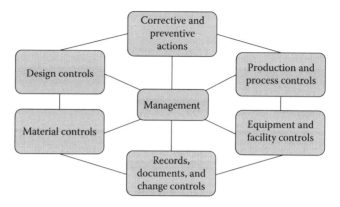

**FIGURE 3.6**
FDA QSIT structure.

4. Corrective and Preventive Actions
5. Material Controls
6. Equipment and Facility Controls
7. Records, Documents, and Change Controls
8. Marketing and Sales

We should note as well that the FDA has emphasized the connection of additional regulatory requirements (Medical Device Reporting,[8] Corrections and Removals,[9] and Medical Device Tracking[10]) with the Quality System Regulation CAPA Subsystem (See Figure 3.7).

Table 3.1 indicates in detail how the sections and subsections of 21 CFR 820 are intended to relate to the QSIT model. Of course, adoption of the QSIT framework does not require agreement with the details of the table.

## ISO 13485 Framework

The ISO 13485 framework is an approach introduced with the general QMS standard ISO 9001:2000, adopted for ISO 13485:2003 and continued with the next revision as ISO 13485:2016. As indicated in Figure 3.8, this approach emphasizes the interactions of business processes to achieve desired results.

---

[8] 21 CFR 803, Medical Device Reporting.
[9] 21 CFR 806, Medical Devices; Reports of Corrections and Removals.
[10] 21 CFR 821, Medical Device Tracking Requirements.

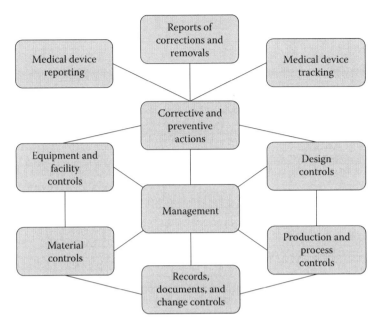

**FIGURE 3.7**
Augmented FDA QSIT approach.

## ISO 9001:2015/Annex SL Framework

With the publication of Annex SL in 2012, the Technical Management Board of ISO declared an objective of delivering consistent and compatible Management System Standards. This document also defines a structure determined more appropriate for harmonization of multiple management system standards than the structure defined in ISO 9001:2000. The structure of Annex SL is the structure used in ISO 9001:2015. A medical device company dedicated to conformity with other management standards (such as ISO 14001, Environmental management systems) may choose to use the structure of ISO 9001:2015/Annex SL because virtually all future QMS standards will use this structure.[11] Appendix B provides guidance for a medical device company that chooses to implement multiple management systems and wishes to accommodate the structure of management standards based on Annex SL.

---

[11] The next revision of ISO 13485 after the revision of 2016 should have the Annex SL structure, but this will surely be some years in the future, and in fact the next revision possibly may not have the Annex SL structure.

**TABLE 3.1**

FDA QSIT Structure[12]

| QSIT Element | 21 CFR 820 Section |
|---|---|
| Management Controls Subsystem | • Management responsibility, 820.20<br>• Quality policy, 820.20(a)<br>• Organization, 820.20(b)<br>• Responsibility and authority, 820.20(b)(1)<br>• Resources, 820.20(b)(2)<br>• Management representative, 820.20(b)(3)<br>• Management review, 820.20(c)<br>• Quality planning, 820.20(d)<br>• Quality system procedures, 820.20(e)<br>• Quality audit, 820.22<br>• Personnel, 820.25 |
| Design Controls Subsystem | • Design controls, 820.30<br>• General, 820.30(a)<br>• Design and development planning, 820.30(b)<br>• Design input, 820.30(c)<br>• Design output, 820.30(d)<br>• Design review, 820.30(e)<br>• Design verification, 820.30(f)<br>• Design validation, 820.30(g)<br>• Design transfer, 820.30(h)<br>• Design changes, 820.30(i)<br>• Device labeling, 820.120<br>• Device packaging, 820.130<br>• Production and process methods and tests, 820.70 & 820.80 |
| Corrective and Preventive Action Subsystem | • Corrective and preventive action, 820.100<br>• Complaints, 820.198<br>• Servicing, 820.200<br>• Acceptance activities, 820.80<br>• Monitoring and control of processes, 820.70(a)(2)<br>• Nonconforming product, 820.90<br>• Control of nonconformities, 820.90(a)<br>• Review and disposition, 820.90(b) |

(*Continued*)

---

[12] Personal communication, fax from Georgia Layloff, FDA.

**TABLE 3.1 (*Continued*)**

FDA QSIT Structure

| QSIT Element | 21 CFR 820 Section |
|---|---|
| Production and Process Controls Subsystem | • General, 820.70(a)<br>• Personnel, 820.70(d)<br>• Manufacturing material, 820.70(h)<br>• Automated processes, 820.70(i)<br>• Process validation, 820.75<br>• Acceptance activities, 820.80<br>• General, 820.80(a)<br>• In-process acceptance, 820.80(c)<br>• Final acceptance, 820.80(d)<br>• Statistical techniques, 820.250<br>• Device labeling, 820.120<br>• Device packaging, 820.130<br>• Installation, 820.170<br>• Servicing, 820.200 |
| Records, Documents and Change Control Subsystem | • General records, 820.180<br>• Design history file, 820.30(j)<br>• Device history record, 820.184<br>• Device master record, 820.181<br>• Quality system record, 820.186<br>• Document controls, 820.40<br>• Document approval & distribution, 820.40(a)<br>• Document changes, 820.40(b)<br>• Production and process changes, 820.70(b) |
| Facilities and Equipment Controls Subsystem | • Buildings, 820.70(f)<br>• Equipment, 820.70(g)<br>• Measuring equipment, 820.72<br>• Environmental control, 820.70(c)<br>• Contamination control, 820.70(e) |
| Material Controls Subsystem | • Purchasing controls, 820.50<br>• Evaluation of suppliers, 820.50(a)<br>• Purchasing data, 820.50(b)<br>• Receiving acceptance activities, 820.80(b)<br>• Identification, 820.60<br>• Traceability, 820.65<br>• Handling, 820.140<br>• Storage, 820.150<br>• Distribution, 820.160<br>• Acceptance status, 820.186<br>• Statistical techniques, 820.250 |

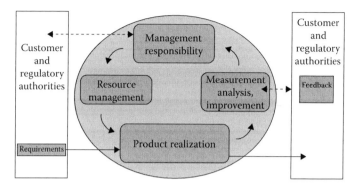

**FIGURE 3.8**
ISO 13485 Process Model. (Adapted from Figure 1 of ANSI/AAMI/ISO TIR 14969:2004.)[13]

## Essentially Two Choices

A pharmaceutical company also making medical devices may choose the FDA CGMP structure. A medical device company implementing multiple management standards may choose the Annex SL structure.

However, for most medical device companies, two choices dominate the landscape:

1. The FDA QSIT framework
2. The ISO 13485 framework

Either can work well.

We can see graphically how either can work by considering the QMS in a little more detail. The ISO 13485 quality standard requires identification of key processes for the company. This is also a good practice for companies whose only regulatory concern is the FDA. Let's assume we have identified our key processes as the following:

- Management Responsibility
- Risk Management
- Documentation Management
- Records Management
- Internal and External Audits
- Qualification and Training

---

[13] ANSI/AAMI/ISO TIR14969:2004 Medical devices—Quality management systems—Guidance on the application of ISO 13485:2003 © 2017 by the Association for the Advancement of Medical Instrumentation.

- Facilities and Equipment
- Software and Process Validation
- Design Control
- Supplier Quality Management
- Product Regulatory Compliance
- Production
- Inspection, Test, Disposition
- Handling, Storage, Preservation, Delivery
- Service and Support
- Marketing and Sales
- Change Control
- Customer Feedback Management
- Corrective and Preventive Action
- Control of Nonconforming Product

Although this is a list that we will use throughout this book, there is nothing special about it. The intent is to separate the management of quality into a moderate number of key processes so that we can then watch over each process to ensure its effective implementation. Any other list, a little longer or a little shorter, that encompasses all the needed processes affecting quality outcomes will do just as well.

These processes can fit either the FDA or the ISO framework.

Figure 3.9 illustrates how this list of key processes will fit within the eight subsystems of the QSIT framework (the subsystems defined by the FDA plus the one that we added, Marketing and Sales).

This same list of key processes will also fit the ISO framework (see Figure 3.10).

How then should we choose?

## Choosing Between FDA and ISO Frameworks

There are reasons both for and against choosing an FDA Framework.

- For
  - The FDA is clearly the most widely respected (read "feared") regulatory agency in the world. It may be prudent to be able emphasize to FDA investigators that the company is taking FDA concerns very seriously.
  - The QSIT framework is well conceived, with the various subsystems often matching well with a company's organization.

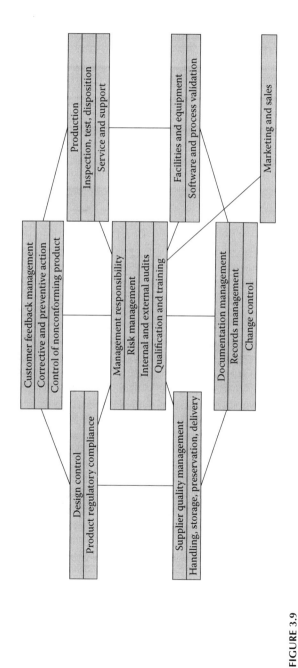

**FIGURE 3.9**

Key Processes within a QSIT framework.

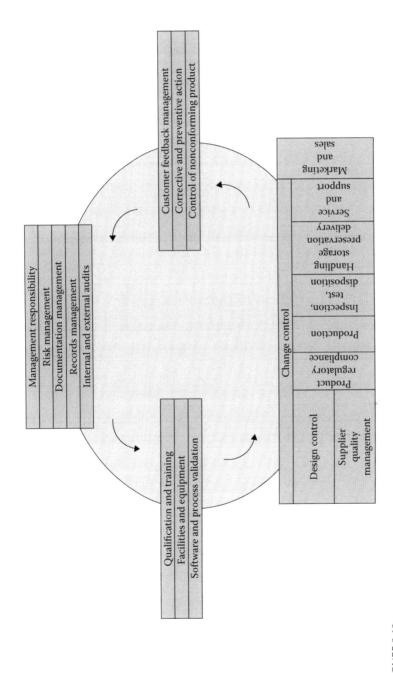

**FIGURE 3.10**
Key Processes within an ISO framework.

- Against
  - As noted in Chapter 1, an increasing number of countries are adopting ISO 13485 as a fundamental component of their regulatory approach. Some of these countries require audits focused on their specific requirements. Use of an FDA Framework may ultimately require more extensive discussions with these external auditors to be able to show that country requirements are being met.[14]
  - For multinational companies where the United States operations are simply one among many important country operations, it may appear inappropriate to employees around the world to have a QMS constructed according to the regulatory approach of one country when a framework based on an international standard would seem more appropriate.

Similarly, there are reasons both for and against an ISO Framework.

- For
  - ISO 13485 is an international standard. Therefore, its framework is a logical choice for any international company.
  - ISO 13485 is based on a process approach to quality management systems – an approach that is highly beneficial to sound functioning of the QMS.
  - ISO 13485 includes business elements explicitly. (A regulatory agency does not concern itself with whether a company has any sales. It is only concerned that the sales it has are of good products.)
  - In principle, a framework based on the ISO 13485 model should facilitate harmonization with other management standards. Regrettably, current status of various international standards indicates that this will not be true for perhaps at least another decade.[15]

---

[14] See Chapter 5 for recommendations on ensuring full coverage of requirements of standards and regulations within the documentation.

[15] As noted earlier, with the publication of Annex SL in 2012, the Technical Management Board of ISO has declared an objective of delivering consistent and compatible Management System Standards. Unfortunately for medical device companies, its immediate effect will be a divergence in structure between ISO 9001:2015 (which has the new structure of Annex SL) and the new revision of ISO 13485 (which retains the basic structure of ISO 13485:2003). Thus, any medical device companies wishing to maintain certification to both standards will find this effort more challenging in the immediate future.

- Against
  - Because the standard was drafted with the original intent to allow exclusion of items in Clause 7 only,[16] there is some separation of items that might more appropriately be addressed together. (For example, it appears artificial that section 8.2.6, Monitoring and measurement of product, is separated from section 7.5, Product realization.)
  - Although ISO auditors provide a valuable service to the companies that they audit and often identify key issues that need to be addressed, FDA investigators represent an organization that can shut down a business or bar products from entering the United States. One school of thought believes that this means all effort should be focused first on the FDA and everything else should be subordinate.

A few conclusions are logical.

- A small- or medium-sized company with facilities only in the United States and no expectation of expanding beyond its borders should choose either the FDA or the ISO Framework, depending upon whichever seems more appropriate for the company and its approach to operations.
- An international company should normally choose the ISO Framework as a visible commitment to an international approach to quality management. This structure allows employees around the world to feel more a part of the system.
- An international company currently finding itself in difficulties with the FDA (such as having received a Warning Letter) may find it useful to be able to demonstrate a sincere commitment to fulfillment of FDA requirements. If the difficulties have indicated issues throughout the QMS, a full reconstruction of the QMS may be the correct approach. In such a case, it may be useful to move to an FDA framework for the remodeled system.
- With the growing number of instances of combination products (drug and medical device) there will be an increasing need to be able to demonstrate fulfillment of all applicable requirements. As noted above, a drug company also selling devices may wish to construct a

---

[16] ISO 13485:2016 allows exclusions for nonapplicable requirements in Clauses 6, 7, and 8.

QMS based on the FDA CGMP guidance with appropriate device requirements added. Appendix A provides details that can assist in identifying gaps to fill for quality management systems for combination products.

As noted earlier, with regard to the decision on level of control, it may be appropriate to plan for a gradually increasing level of control over a period of years. The decision on framework is different. The framework, once initially established, is likely to become ingrained in employees. It will be changed only with difficulty and thus deserves careful attention at the start.

Once decisions on level of control and framework have been made, it is time to create the quality plan.

# 4

## A Quality Plan

## BACKGROUND TO THE PLAN

We know our company. We know its organization and its culture. We know its vision for the kind of company it wants to be. We know its products and the markets it wants to serve (and thus the applicable regulations). Some key decisions have been made, such as:

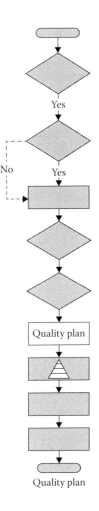

- We have decided on the extent of centralized control, guided by company culture and what seems likely to provide the best opportunities for the business.
- Part of that decision has been the determination whether to seek a single QMS or several, or perhaps to work progressively toward a single system.
- We know whether the framework is to be the U.S. Food and Drug Administration (FDA) QSIT (Quality System Inspection Technique) structure or the International Organization for Standardization (ISO) process model—or possibly a customized approach to our particular company.
- And if we plan to sell combination products, we know our QMS will need to include extra elements based on the regulations for all applicable product types.

With all this in mind, we are ready to prepare the quality plan to create (or re-create) our QMS.

---

## QUALITY PLAN

The journey to an effective and efficient QMS must begin with a plan. As mentioned earlier, senior management must support the effort if it is to succeed. A quality plan is essential so that both senior management and the quality/regulatory organization have a clear view of the goal and the path for reaching that goal.

Even if management is fully convinced of the value of a more effective QMS and have initiated the process themselves, a quality plan is still the needed first step. Going beyond senior management and the quality/regulatory organization, the plan provides a vehicle for communication throughout the organization. Once approved, the plan should be shared widely at all levels in the company. The quality plan should include the following components:[1]

- The objectives to be accomplished
- The scope, both geographically and organizationally
- Resources required
- Actions to be taken with clear indication of who is responsible
- Timeline
- Approvals

Within that general structure, the plan should include a few key subject areas:

- Documentation transitioning
- Human resources
- Software infrastructure

---

## DOCUMENTATION TRANSITIONING

In the real world, of course, the construction of an effective QMS does not start with a blank slate (unless the company is a startup). There is always a collection of documentation already in effect with which employees, to varying extents, are familiar.

---

[1] There is an international standard for quality plans: ISO 10005:2005, "Quality management systems—Guidelines for quality plans." However, this standard "is focused primarily on product realization and is not a guide to organizational quality management system planning."

In some instances, it is the complexity of that documentation that created the impetus for making changes. Nevertheless, it is not usually the best move to try to wipe the slate clean entirely and start over fresh.

Although employees are often exhorted to "embrace change," few are able to do this readily. Change is disturbing to most people; the plan should try to leave alone as much as possible. The following can be a useful sequence to incorporate into the plan; it means basically starting at the top of the documentation pyramid and working down.[2]

- Start with a new quality manual (as well as a new quality policy if appropriate). Particularly if employees all receive personal copies they will see the new focus on quality and will see their own places in the big picture.
- If there is an existing Level 2 documentation, leave the name of that documentation as it is. (These documents may be called Standard Operating Procedures, Quality System Policies, Quality Procedures, or some other designation.) The name for this documentation is not critical; its content is.[3] The number of these procedures needs to be something reasonable, certainly fewer than 30.[4] If there is a lot of detail regarding the "how" for required actions in the existing procedures, this material needs to be moved to Level 3. In the course of working on the Level 2 documentation, department heads will have an opportunity to be reminded of all the key requirements affecting their departments.
- In tackling the normally large number of Level 3 documents, department heads must play a key role. If prioritization becomes an issue for resources in making changes to Level 3 documentation, first priority should be given to processes involving customers and patient safety, such as complaints and adverse-event reporting.

All of this activity represents a quite significant bolus of effort near the start, and the plan will need to give careful attention to the resources required. The plan needs to assure that the ongoing business is maintained while the improvements are being implemented behind the scenes.

---

[2] An alternative approach is to start with the Level 2 procedures, since this permits references at specific places in the manual to the relevant Level 2 procedures. At a minimum, in drafting the manual, the drafters must know in general terms the structure and content of Level 2.

[3] See Chapter 7 and Appendix C for more detail regarding Level 2.

[4] As an example, see Chapter 3 for a suggested list of 20 identified processes that can serve as subjects for Level 2 procedures.

───────

## HUMAN RESOURCES

### Quality Council

A key message for the success of the QMS is: "Quality is everyone's business." Establishment of a quality council is a valuable contribution for making this message a reality.

Although the management review process is intended to ensure appropriate oversight of the QMS at the senior management level, the frequency of such reviews, whether annual, semiannual, or quarterly, does not provide the month-to-month attention that the QMS needs on an ongoing basis—particularly when making major improvements. For this, some version of a quality council is needed. As noted earlier, the steering committee may transition into a quality council; alternatively, the quality plan should address its establishment. For a multisite company, it is often useful to have a quality council at each site, in addition to a coordinating quality council for the whole company.

In the ideal case, each site should have a quality council with representatives from middle-management of each department (not just from quality/regulatory departments).[5] Initially, the council should oversee the implementation of the quality plan for overhaul of the QMS at the site and should meet at least monthly. In the long run the group will be needed for general oversight, ongoing review of the metrics indicating the health of the QMS and identifying and implementing annual quality objectives under the oversight of the senior management team. At this later stage, it may be enough to meet every two months.

A quality council is also the best group to oversee the assembly of information for management review to ensure that appropriate issues are brought to the attention of senior management, usually with options and recommendations from the council as to how to address those issues.

As noted above, in multisite companies to get full benefit from the establishment of a QMS across the organization, a quality council with representation from throughout the organization is needed. This council will initially focus on implementation of the quality plan across the whole company, but in the long run will address multisite issues that arise. As the QMS matures, this "global" quality council will probably find it useful

───────

[5] If the site head is particularly dedicated to the effective implementation of the QMS, it is possible for the quality council to be composed of those reporting to the site head.

to establish multisite teams to encourage consistent behavior across sites in areas such as internal audits, CAPA, and validation. As at the site level, a "global" quality council is the group to oversee preparation of information for management review at the global level, ensuring that important issues are brought to management with options and recommendations for resolving those issues.

## QMS Support Staff

Both the Quality System Regulation and the ISO 13485 quality system standard require designation of a management representative to be responsible for certain tasks, including:

- Ensuring establishment and maintenance of QMS requirements
- Promoting awareness of regulatory and customer requirements
- Identifying QMS processes and ensuring their execution
- Reporting on performance of the QMS to senior management

Focusing of this responsibility on one individual is appropriate. Nevertheless, the person designated as management representative is often the most senior quality and/or regulatory person at the site, who therefore has many other responsibilities.

It may be possible for the management representative to delegate assignments to members of the quality council. However, quality council members also have full-time positions that require their focused attention on a day-to-day basis. Since their positions relate to specific departments, they naturally see issues from a departmental point of view.

In order for the QMS to contribute full value to the company, the QMS needs to have advocates for the big picture. This often means a need to establish a group (or in the case of a small company, perhaps just a single person) to assist the management representative with oversight of the QMS on a day-to-day basis.

Such a group becomes, in effect, a secretariat for the quality council and may be assigned tasks, such as:

- Ensuring that the QMS keeps pace with changes in regulations and standards worldwide
- Collecting and assessing key QMS process metrics
- Overseeing internal audits
- Planning and developing modules for QMS training

In larger, multisite companies such a group becomes even more important. Tasks assigned may include, in addition to the above:

- Promoting consistency of key processes across sites
- Guiding resolution of intersite issues
- Ensuring that issues identified in an external audit at one site are addressed if necessary at other sites
- Overseeing the planning and execution of QMS software for all sites of the business

## SOFTWARE INFRASTRUCTURE

Good software for managing QMS processes in conjunction with other business processes can be critical for an efficient and effective quality system. In the twenty-first century, a company with a QMS with processes that are implemented through an integrated system of software applications will be at a competitive advantage compared to companies with processes carried out with paper (or with a multitude of electronic systems that do not communicate with each other).

Although some companies may be intimidated by regulations related to electronic records, most software applications available are now designed to be validated as compliant with regulations.[6] Careful attention in the planning will lead to a software infrastructure that can benefit the company for many years.

Software application providers are capable of a wide variety of offerings. QMS process software options include:

- Document control
- Change control
- Training administration, delivery and records
- Audits: internal and supplier
- Corrective and preventive action
- Complaints
- Adverse events

---

[6] This is true as long as the company only configures the application and does not customize. Customization is likely to require more validation effort.

- Product lifecycle management (from the Design History File to Device Master Record and beyond)
- Risk management
- Supplier evaluation and management
- Nonconformities and deviations
- Process metrics and reports
- Submissions management
- Calibration and maintenance
- Cost of quality
- Clinical trials management
- IT service management
- Statistical process control

The sheer variety of opportunities and options available can be bewildering—again placing a high value on devoting sufficient time in the planning process so that the result is an infrastructure contributing to efficiency. At the time of the initial construction/reconstruction of the QMS, it may not be possible to install and validate all of the software infrastructure ultimately desired. Some software applications will have to be delayed for future QMS improvement plans. Nevertheless, the ultimate expected structure should be part of the vision going into this plan.

In prioritizing, a good software application for document management should be at the top of the list, and because records of training on procedures are critical, a software application to manage training is a good companion to the documentation software. After that, corrective and preventive action (CAPA) should be considered as next in line, because a good CAPA system allows straightforward tracking of corrective actions for problems found, as well as preventive actions for improving the operation of the QMS. Complaint and adverse event handling (customer feedback management) is a third item that deserves to be among the highest priorities for software applications.

Integration of software application modules is important in a variety of areas; each company will need to prioritize both the installation of modules and their integration.

- Documentation integrated with training facilitates training on procedure changes.
- Training integrated with human resources ensures that as employees come on board, their training needs can be planned

and when they leave, their training records can be appropriately archived.

- CAPA should be integrated with systems that may identify problems requiring corrective action, such as complaints, audits (internal, external, and supplier) and nonconformity management.
- Risk management should be integrated with product lifecycle management, supplier quality, change control, process validation, complaints, and adverse events.

The quality plan needs to ensure that adequate time is taken to manage the implementation of QMS software. Taking shortcuts will almost always lead to problems down the road. The plan needs to include adequate time for:

- Identification and validation of requirements
- Evaluation of potential suppliers[7]
- Installation and validation
- Training

It is always tempting to reduce the time for creating the requirements document and evaluating possible suppliers; the temptation should be resisted.

## APPROVAL

When the quality plan for improvement of the QMS is complete, it needs appropriate approval. This means that approval must include more than simply the head of quality/regulatory. If the plan is approved by the president and/or the heads of departments with responsibility for the actions to be taken, implementation will be much more straightforward than if the plan is perceived as a plan owned by the quality/regulatory organization. Approval of the plan thus reinforces the concept that "quality is everyone's business."

With the plan in place we can begin its fulfillment.

---

[7] If internal development of the software is considered, particular attention must be given to the long-term maintenance and change control of the software application.

# 5

# Documentation, the Big Picture

Good documentation is at the core of an effective quality management system (QMS); it is a good place to begin.

The actions of people are ultimately what decide whether a QMS accomplishes its goals, and those actions depend upon documentation that is understandable and straightforward. People want to do the right thing, but if they have to struggle to figure out what they are supposed to do, they will lose patience and do whatever seems sensible (which may or may not correspond with the documentation).

An ongoing effort will be needed to keep the number of procedures at a minimum and to ensure that the same subject matter is not addressed by multiple procedures. As problems arise, possibly identified by internal or external audits, the temptation is to write new procedures to deal with them. As noted earlier, in some companies it is easier to create a new procedure than it is to amend a procedure already on the books. The consequence is a proliferation of procedures with overlapping applicability, a source for entirely new kinds of problems down the road.

Ultimately, however, the most critical aspect is that employees must be able to determine readily those procedures that are applicable to their work. A well-planned documentation system can make this possible.

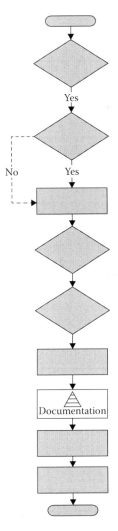

Documentation

## STRUCTURE

The traditional structure for QMS documentation, shown earlier in Figure 3.1, has proven its value in making quality management systems effective.

The apex of the documentation pyramid contains the most fundamental statements of company policies for quality and regulatory concerns. This 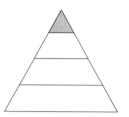 normally includes both the Quality Policy and the Quality Manual. These should be written in clear language so that employees, when reading these documents, can see how their work fits into the big picture of the QMS as a whole. See Chapter 6 for a more detailed discussion of Level 1 documentation.

Level 2 of the pyramid contains procedures that 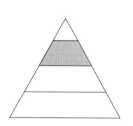 state in more explicit terms what must be done and who is responsible to do it (and at times when it must be done). This should be a relatively small number of procedures (less than thirty) that cover all the key processes of the QMS. Most employees are involved in only a few of these processes. Therefore, by focusing on these few procedures, employees can get a clear picture of the principles that they are expected to apply in their daily activities. See Chapter 7 for a discussion of Level 2 documentation and Appendix C for examples.

Level 3 procedures address the details of how 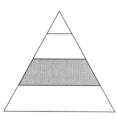 those principles are supposed to be executed for the company. These procedures need to be written in a way that eliminates any ambiguities with regard to expectations. See Chapter 8 for a discussion of Level 3 documentation and Appendices D and E for examples.

Finally, the fourth level of documentation 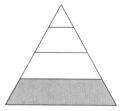 includes the records showing fulfillment of the requirements spelled out in the other three levels. It is often used as the formal home for other documentation related to the QMS. See Chapter 9 for a discussion of Level 4 documentation.

When these concepts are well executed, employees can see the big picture in the top level. They can see the key principles affecting their work in the second level, and they can see the details of how they are sup-posed to carry out their responsibilities in the third level. The records of evidence that they have fulfilled responsibilities are maintained in the fourth level.

In most cases, each Level 2 procedure will have multiple Level 3 proce-dures established to fulfill its requirements.

- At one extreme would be the area of production. There may be a single Level 2 procedure governing production. All procedures for making the company's products are related Level 3 procedures.
- At another extreme may be a Level 2 procedure for the area of management responsibility. One can imagine sufficient specificity for management review in the Level 2 procedure so that a Level 3 procedure may not even be necessary to ensure fulfillment of requirements.

Just as icons at the start of each paragraph above provide a graphical high-light of the documentation level, so also have some companies chosen to help employees readily identify the level of documentation on each docu-ment. A small appropriately shaded pyramid icon in the header or footer can help employees see at a glance the intended level of documentation.

A smart numbering system can also help employees to know at a glance the level of a document. Smart numbers can also help employees to know the relationships between Level 2 and Level 3, and between Level 3 and the applicable forms.

## RIGHT NUMBER OF LEVELS

There is of course no regulation or standard that requires a specific num-ber of documentation levels, or that stipulates what is required content of each level. Nevertheless, it is usually best, even within a small company, to maintain a distinction between Level 2 and Level 3 procedures.

For small single-site companies there is a temptation to "simplify" by having a single set of procedures, plus a manual. If all of the basic require-ments for what and who can be included in the manual, and the manual is still readable, this approach may work. More commonly the tendency is to use a more basic manual and then mix the features of Level 2 and Level 3.

The result is a set of procedures attempting to address the what, the who, and the how. This tends to lead to a glazing over of employees' eyes as they try to absorb this complex mixture.

---

## FORMAT

Too often, procedures are planned from the point of view of the person writing the procedure. More important is the point of view of the persons expected to use the procedure.

Perhaps the most immediate question for any reader picking up a procedure is: "Does this procedure apply to me?" Procedures should be designed to make the answer to this question easy.

- This begins with the title. Titles should be as short as possible, but long enough to communicate the basic subject matter being addressed. Users have to deal with long lists of procedures; if titles in the lists are truly informative they do not usually have to look at a procedure itself to determine whether it is of interest.
- It is logical to begin each procedure with a purpose statement. However, temptation should be resisted to turn this section into an essay. Keep it simple.
- The next statement should be a scope statement. This is the statement that provides the answer to the question of applicability. It should state briefly the subject matter for the procedure, going into a little more detail than the title, but even more importantly should indicate the sites and perhaps even specifically the departments that are to be governed by the procedure.
- A responsibility section can be useful in listing the specific departments or positions that have actions for which they are responsible as spelled out in the procedure.

Table 5.1 summarizes some typical procedure elements. The order listed is typical for procedures designed by quality and regulatory professionals. Those coming from other backgrounds are likely to prefer the procedure section itself much earlier in the procedure, directly after the scope statement, to get to the action sooner.[1] The order chosen is less critical than

---

[1] My personal preference is to get to the action of the procedure as soon as possible.

ensuring that each procedure of a particular type is formatted in the same way. The reader needs to know in what order to expect the elements of each procedure.

**TABLE 5.1**

Procedure Elements

| Element | Comment |
|---|---|
| Title | Should be informative. When appearing in a list of procedures, the title should be capable of indicating what it is actually about. Note that it is pointless to include the word "procedure" in the title of a procedure. |
| Purpose | Brief statement of the goals for the procedure |
| Scope | Both subject matter and organizational applicability. It may be useful to address what is not in scope. |
| Responsibility | This section identifies departments, or even specific positions, responsible for carrying out the actions of the procedure. There is some risk that this section can become a second procedure section; effort will be required to keep it succinct. |
| References | This must include documents (external and internal) referenced elsewhere in the procedure and should include other important references. Since keeping these references up to date is a significant ongoing concern, the "other important references" should be kept to a minimum. |
| Glossary | Acronyms used in the document must be defined. |
| | Terms with specific quality or regulatory meaning must also be defined, as well as terms that may be unique to the company. |
| | It is generally useful to use FDA definitions of terms when multiple definitions are available. An important exception is the FDA use of the term "correction," which the FDA uses to refer to a product recall action in the field, whereas more general usage is to refer to fixing a problem without necessarily fixing the root cause of the problem.[2] |
| | A particular challenge is ensuring that terms are defined the same from one procedure to the next. It is useful to have a master list for the glossary. |
| Materials and Equipment | Generally applicable only to certain types of Level 3 procedures |
| Warnings/ Precautions | If there are any, this section should be in bold type or otherwise highlighted and should appear just prior to the procedure section. |
| Procedure | The core of the procedure. See Appendix C for examples of Level 2 procedures, and see Appendices D and E for examples of Level 3 procedures. |

*(Continued)*

---

[2] See Appendix C, Corrective and Preventive Action.

**TABLE 5.1 (*Continued*)**

Procedure Elements

| Element | Comment |
| --- | --- |
| Records | The existence of a procedure normally implies that there must result some objective evidence that the procedure was carried out as intended. Thus, particularly for Level 3 procedures, it is useful to state in the procedure what are the resulting required records and where those records are maintained. |
| Attachments | Generally used for information important to the procedure that would detract from the flow if inserted into the body of the procedure. Some companies include forms related to the procedure, but this has the disadvantage that a change to one requires a change to both. |
| Revision History | Unless the procedure has been completely rewritten from beginning to end, this section should indicate exactly what has changed from the prior version to the current version so that the reader can quickly learn what must be done differently. The effectiveness date for each revision should also be prominent on the document. |
| Approvals | Under normal circumstances, the head of each department responsible for actions in the procedure should be a required approver for the procedure. The reader should be able to see who has approved the procedure. In this manner employees can see that the head of their department has approved the procedures they are using. If approvals come only from the quality/regulatory function, implementation is quicker but less effective in the long run. |
| | It should be added that there may be procedures requiring regulatory approval even when the procedure does not govern the regulatory function. For example, persons with responsibility for regulatory submissions in the various countries should have responsibility to review design control and change control procedures to ensure those procedures fulfill requirements. |
| Headers/ Footers | Routine data: Company name and/or logo, procedure title, procedure number, revision indication, page number. Most companies use the format "page x of y," but an equally satisfactory alternative is for the last page of the procedure to state at the end "last page." Headers or footers are also appropriate homes for icons indicating documentation level as described earlier. |

## CAUTIONS

### Flexibility

It may be tempting to allow considerable flexibility within a procedure as a means of empowering employees and encouraging them to take ownership of the QMS. Although the intent of such an approach is laudable, experience indicates that most employees prefer exercising their creativity in areas outside of the QMS. Most appear to have an attitude along the lines of "Just tell me what to do, so I can do it and get on with what I really care about."

At the same time, many procedures benefit from an explicit mechanism for authorizing exceptions, normally requiring quality and/or regulatory approval. This can allow processes to proceed in a near normal manner when something a little out of the ordinary occurs. It allows for a commonsense resolution of issues with appropriate quality and/or regulatory review and approval.

## Language

In choosing the vocabulary used in procedures, companies should use the words that employees use in their everyday work. Regulations and standards routinely use the word "device" because of the need for precision in usage. However, in most companies, employees are accustomed to call the items they design, manufacture, and sell "products." Company procedures in those companies should use the word "product" and not the word "device."

Similarly, employees may find that the use of "shall," rather than "must" in procedures seems stilted and off-putting. Although "shall" is used in most regulations and standards, there is no reason not to use "must" in company procedures. Indeed, if usage of "must" makes procedures easier for all to understand, this is a strong argument in favor of using it.

## Content

It is advisable to keep in mind that whatever is required in a procedure (whether Level 1, Level 2, or Level 3) will be audited. Ensure that records created as a result of the procedure will be clear even to an external party.[3]

---

[3] A colleague has reported that it is distressing to sit across the table from an auditor reading the same procedure the auditor is reading and be obliged to wonder "Why did we write this in this manner?"

---

## ELECTRONIC DOCUMENTATION

Electronic control of documentation is the only practical approach for the twenty-first century. There should be few exceptions to electronic documents, such as hard copies of the quality policy and the quality manual as discussed in Chapter 6.

With electronic document management, the current official version is always the document that the employee pulls up on the computer each day. Printed versions may be authorized for use under specific circumstances, such as the day of printing.

Electronic approvals (fulfilling applicable regulatory requirements) provide additional benefits. Approvers in an electronic approval system normally do not have the extensive possibilities for wordsmithing that are available with hardcopy approvals. This can lead to fewer rounds of approval and shorter document cycle times. If the document management system displays the approval date along with the name of the approver, then all employees using that procedure can see which approver delayed longest in approving. This feature may also help to provide shorter document cycle times.

---

## COVERING ALL MARKETS

Regulatory authorities around the world do recognize that greater harmonization of regulatory requirements worldwide will make it easier for companies to establish effective quality management systems for all jurisdictions. However, the natural and unfortunate tendency is for each authority to approach the harmonization process with the attitude: "Be reasonable: Do it my way."

Nevertheless, progress is being made. The International Medical Device Regulators Forum (IMDRF, at www.imdrf.org) has recognized regulatory harmonization as a goal. Even though we recognize that progress is being made, in constructing the documentation for our QMS, we cannot afford to wait.

While we are waiting (and working) for international harmonization, the approach indicated by Annex A of the Canadian Guidance, GD210, provides logical guidance for companies in designing their quality management systems—not only for Canada, but more generally.

First, ensure that the requirements in ISO 13485 are addressed in the QMS documentation. Then, in addition, ensure provisions for the multiple legitimate concerns that each country will have. These include the following:

- There must be records that show top management's commitment to fulfill requirements and for the company to maintain the most current regulatory information for the country/region. Changes to regulatory requirements in any country where the company sells products should be updated and documented as part of the management review process.
- There must be objective evidence that the company is fully aware of product approval requirements for the country/region. (This should not normally mean a separate procedure for each country/region, but rather should be some combination of training for regulatory staff, vetting of outsourced regulatory services, and spreadsheets or databases documenting requirements country by country. The documentation should also include copies of the applicable regulations and/or evidence that the outsourced service has access to the applicable regulations.)
- Processes must be in place to ensure that only product approved for the market can be shipped to the country/region.
- Processes must be in place in the country/region for complaint handling, adverse-event reporting, and recalls if needed.
- Distribution records for the country must be available that allow effective recalls if required, including any additional detail required for tracking implantable devices or other special traceability requirements.
- Definitions: Country/regional definitions are not likely to be in serious conflict with definitions in the standards, but where they differ, the local definitions will be applied by regulatory authorities. Particular attention must be paid to the term "manufacturer," which in some jurisdictions is not the company that actually produced the device, but rather is the company that places the product on the market.
- Particularly for countries where extremes of temperature and humidity are common, there must be evidence of adequate provision for transportation and storage.

- Design changes must be addressed in a manner that ensures compliance with local regulations (possible need for reregistration).
- Labeling must fulfill country/regional requirements. Canadian authorities are particularly concerned to verify that documentation is fully aligned on the ISO 13485 certificate, the product license, and the labeling. It is prudent to provide for this level of alignment for all markets where product is intended to be sold.
- Internal audits must address the worldwide requirements, and how they are being fulfilled.
- Clinical trials held in a country/region must be carried out in accordance with local regulations.

The last step of adapting documentation to markets around the world will be the fine tuning. For this, we must review the details of requirements in each country where we want to sell products.

Recent documents for the Medical Device Single Audit Program (MDSAP), one of the work items of the IMDRF, provide valuable assistance with the fine tuning.[4] MDSAP is a program intended to allow participating companies to plan for a single audit each year that addresses routine concerns for participating regulatory authorities (Australia, Brazil, Canada, Japan, and the United States) instead of the possibility of multiple audits on behalf of these authorities.[5] This audit model, although less detailed than the Canadian Guidance GD210, nevertheless addresses explicitly the QMS regulatory requirements for each participating country that go beyond the requirements of ISO 13485.

This is the point where we add in the details such as the Mercado Común del Sur (MERCOSUR)/Brazilian requirement that not only the design output but the design history file must be approved by signature and date. For variations on normally accepted practice, such as this, there may be a temptation to specify the requirement only in relation to products for those countries having the requirement. However, this can lead to dangerous complexity in the QMS. The best approach is a single set of practices that are applied universally. In the case of this specific practice, it is a good practice. Many businesses have found value in audits of their

---

[4] MDSAP Medical Device Single Audit Program, Audit Model, MDSAP AU P0002.004 2017-01-06 and MDSAP Medical Device Single Audit Program, Companion Document, MDSAP AU G0002.1.004 2017-01-06 revised 2017-04-13.

[5] Although this is an international program, information about this program is available at the FDA website. Go to www.fda.gov and search for MDSAP.

design history files (DHF) at the end of development, and it is appropriate to tie signature approval of the DHF to the audit results.

## ENSURING FULL COVERAGE

After creating the documentation, we need to be sure that we have addressed all of the pieces we think we have. This requires additional effort, worthwhile just for peace of mind. Moreover, there is a practical benefit because the exercise results in tables that are useful for external audits.

It is the responsibility of the quality or regulatory department to ensure that all applicable requirements from regulations and standards are appropriately addressed within the QMS. The best way to ensure this is to create spreadsheets along the lines of that indicated in Figure 5.1.

Such a spreadsheet extends for many more rows (over 120) to accommodate all of the Quality System Regulation, and may cover other FDA regulations as well. It is important to include most of the wording in each item listed in column 1, because without these details it is very easy to review the company procedures too quickly. One can allow oneself to believe that the requirements of the regulation are covered when they are not.

A similar spreadsheet should be created for ISO 13485, although in preparing and using such a spreadsheet, it is important to remember that some copyright issues apply for ISO 13485 that do not apply for the Quality System Regulation.

It will also be useful to prepare a third spreadsheet that addresses other worldwide regulatory requirements for the QMS in the same manner. Such a spreadsheet should focus on those regulatory elements that go beyond the requirements of ISO 13485. A good place to start for identifying those elements is Canadian Guidance Document GD210, augmented by the MDSAP Audit Model. What Canada and the other MDSAP participants expect is usually expected in other countries, although ensuring the dependability of this third spreadsheet requires examination of QMS requirements for each country where products are to be sold.

To fill out each row of the table, it is important to be as specific as possible. For example, it is not appropriate just to check in each box that the manual addresses such and such a requirement. Rather the specific page or section of the manual should be identified. Similarly for the Level 2

| 21CFR 820 | Manual | Level 2 | Level 3 |
|---|---|---|---|
| 820.5 Quality system<br>Each manufacturer shall establish and maintain a quality system that is appropriate for the specific medical device(s) designed or manufactured, and that meets the requirements of this part. | | | |
| Management Controls Subsystem | | | |
| 820.20 Management responsibility (title) | | | |
| 820.20(a) Quality policy<br>Management … shall establish its policy and objectives for, and commitment to, quality … shall ensure that the quality policy is understood, implemented, and maintained at all levels of the organization. | | | |
| 820.20(b) Organization<br>Each manufacture shall establish and maintain an adequate organizational structure to ensure that devices are designed and produced in accordance with the requirements of this part. | | | |
| 820.20(b)(1) Responsibility and authority<br>Each manufacturer shall establish the appropriate responsibility, authority, and interrelation of all personnel who manage, perform, and assess work affecting quality, and provide the independence and authority necessary to perform these tasks. | | | |
| 820.20(b)(2) Resources<br>Each manufacturer shall provide adequate resources, including the assignment of trained personnel, for management, performance of work, and assessment activities, including internal quality audits, to meet the requirements of this part. | | | |

**FIGURE 5.1**

Trace matrix for quality system regulation.

procedures, it is likely that only a brief section of a Level 2 procedure will address each row of the table. On the other hand it is possible that the "how-to" details of Level 3 procedures may mean that an entire Level 3 procedure is fully devoted to implementing the requirements of a single row in the table.

Each procedure in the company should find a home in the table, with some exceptions. Procedures that describe how to make products (components of device master records) are not useful inclusions. In addition, there are likely a large number of equipment-specific procedures for calibration and maintenance; these are also not useful inclusions.

When tables have been completed, two key bits of information will be available:

1. It will be clear whether there are any gaps in the coverage. This may be the absence of coverage of a regulatory requirement at any level of the documentation. It may be that the coverage of a requirement is hidden away in a Level 3 procedure that many may be unaware of. It may be that it is addressed in principle in a Level 2 procedure, but there is no Level 3 procedure describing how to implement the requirement. Whatever their nature, these gaps should be filled.

2. It will also be apparent if there is duplication of material in more than one procedure. This can easily happen in Level 3 documents. After conference with the persons using the apparently redundant documents, it will be possible to decide which procedure is the best home for the material. Alternatively, if the decision is that the material needs to have more than one procedural home, the exercise will flag situations where changes in one procedure should trigger assessment of the other procedure addressing the same subject.

Full coverage in the documentation is satisfying for quality and regulatory staff. Indeed, it is critical in surviving, and thriving, through the many audits a company is subject to these days. However, equally important is the way in which this documentation reaches employees. We need to ensure that the documentation has a meaningful impact—in a positive way—on employees. For this we need to consider each documentation level in more detail, as in the next few chapters.

# 6

## Level 1 Documentation

### QUALITY POLICY

The quality policy provides an opportunity for the company to put its commitment to quality in a few words and in a manner that can be readily shared across the whole organization. It should be straightforward and readily understandable, rather than a complex and detailed elaboration of fine points. Table 6.1 provides some examples of quality policies that have been used by medical device companies. Some are quite short; others are more elaborate.

In the ideal case, the points in the quality policy should be memorable so that employees can more readily keep its messages in mind amid the stress and pressures of everyday work. On the other hand, it can be so short that it may have difficulty meeting content requirements (see below).

Many companies have developed statements of mission, vision, and values. The quality policy must be consistent with such statements, but should remain separate. Statements of mission, vision, and values can be appropriately idealistic in tone as an expression for everything the company wants to be. The quality policy, on the other hand, should be closer to reality; it should be a statement of what the company can reasonably expect to achieve.

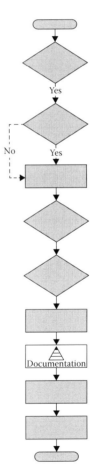

Documentation Level 1

**TABLE 6.1**

Quality Policy Examples (Company Names Omitted)

Improve the Quality of Patient Care and all things [company name].

It is the [company name]'s Quality Policy to improve health care by providing high-quality, safe, and effective diagnostic products.

We, as [company name] employees, are committed to building quality partnerships with our customers and suppliers. We do this by consistently designing, producing, and delivering products and services that meet or exceed our customers' expectations.
We will lead our business processes based on meaningful metrics, and on our dedication to continuously improve our performance and partnerships.

We will exceed our customers' expectations by striving without reserve for unsurpassed product quality, reliability, and patient safety through effective, agile, and compliant processes.
We are committed to maintain and continually improve the effectiveness of our quality management systems, comply with all applicable requirements, and deliver excellence to customers through our products, processes, services, and relationships.

[Company name] is committed to delivering satisfaction to our customers by anticipating their needs and offering value, quality, and reliability that exceeds their expectations.
The success of [company name] and our customers is powered by our people, a culture of teamwork, innovative solutions, and by continually improving the effectiveness of our Quality System as a foundation for business performance.
We value safety, integrity, and mutual respect, supporting our employees, communities, and customers, and complying with all applicable laws and regulations.
This is The [company name] Way, a culture of quality.

Delivering safe and effective life-sustaining products to patients is the most critical aspect of our work. [Company name]'s reputation is built on our ability to consistently provide quality products to the marketplace. To safeguard our customers' trust, every [company name] employee is expected to demonstrate uncompromising dedication to quality.
[Company name] employees are expected to:
- Deliver quality services conforming with the [company name] QMS.
- Act as champions of product quality and quality management systems
- Meet commitments to regulatory authorities.
- Immediately raise quality issues to your supervisor and/or to the appropriate quality personnel.
- Report all product complaints from any source to [appropriate department] within one business day.
- Report all adverse events from any source to [appropriate department] within one business day.
- Fully understand, be trained in, and follow your department's [procedures]. Any confusion on how to properly follow the [procedure] should be brought to the attention of your manager.

## Content

Requirements with regard to the quality policy are of two kinds: content and implementation.

The FDA is vague with regard to content, requiring simply establishment of a quality policy and a commitment to quality, and communication of this throughout the organization. ISO 13485 specifies more detail. The quality policy must: (1) be appropriate to the purpose of the organization; (2) include a commitment to comply with requirements and maintain quality system effectiveness; (3) provide a framework for managing quality objectives; (4) be reviewed periodically for suitability.

An FDA investigator is unlikely to pursue issues related to the content of the quality policy. Questions related to the quality policy in the QSIT guide relate only to establishing its existence and its implementation.[1]

On the other hand, auditors checking fulfillment of ISO 13485 requirements are likely to go into these requirements in some detail. Of course it is highly improbable that a company would implement a quality policy that is somehow inconsistent with the purpose of the organization, so the first requirement is unlikely to attract attention.

However, the wording of the second requirement was specifically aimed at medical device companies and fulfillment of regulatory requirements. Not surprisingly, auditors prefer to see an explicit statement of commitment to fulfilling regulatory requirements. They may accept a statement where the commitment is only implied. For example, a commitment in the quality policy to fulfilling customer requirements may be sufficient if the training materials related to the quality policy make it explicitly clear that regulatory agencies are included among the customers whose requirements are to be fulfilled. Close reading of Table 6.1 suggests that some of these companies may have had to be creative in persuading their registrars that their quality policy meets the second requirement.

Curiously, some auditors have regarded a commitment only to continual improvement of the QMS (without an explicit statement regarding its maintenance) as an inadequate indication of commitment to its maintenance. The logic of that attitude is impossible to comprehend. Nevertheless, in such instances it may also be necessary to ensure that the

---

[1] "Guide to Inspections of Quality Systems," U.S. Food and Drug Administration, August 1999.

related training materials make the criticality of maintaining the QMS clear to all in the company.

The requirement related to management of objectives for quality is an important reason why the quality policy must be realistic, and not idealistic, in its statements. All in the company should be able to see that the company cares enough about the policy to ensure that it is being fulfilled. Each meaningful statement in the policy should have a corresponding related objective. Moreover, auditors may expect that the company is using metrics to determine whether these objectives are being fulfilled.

Although not a requirement, it is beneficial if the quality policy is stated in the first person—sometimes "I" but more commonly "we." When the policy is stated in terms such as "employees must" it takes ownership away from the employees and gives it to company management. This is contrary to the goal of wanting all in the company to take ownership of their share of quality so that "quality is everyone's business."

## Implementation

Implementation of the quality policy is an instance where simple fulfillment of regulatory requirements may fall far short of what can truly be achieved in benefiting the company. To satisfy auditors, it is probably enough to:

- Include the Quality Policy in the quality manual
- Place some posters on the wall
- Regularly visit the subject in quality training sessions

More is needed to gain full value of the quality policy for the company.

In the first place, graphic representations of the quality policy need to have the same level of attention to corporate image that marketing materials receive. If employees see that materials for quality get the same kind of first-class approach as marketing and sales materials, they get a powerful message that the company is really serious about quality. Moreover, if the signature of the company president appears on the graphic representations, the message is that this is important for everyone in the company. If the signature is only that of the vice president for quality, the message is less forceful.

The quality policy, with well-designed graphics consistent with the corporate image, should be printed in several different sizes:

- Large posters for conference rooms—and not just conference rooms used by quality and regulatory staff
- A letter size (8½ × 11) copy for each employee (A4 size for outside the United States)
- Business card–size for wallets and to give away to customers and visitors

Attention to quality is important for the company website (and Facebook page), and the quality policy should be prominent as part of this effort. It was striking to find in research for this book how few companies give prominence to their quality policy on the company website.

## Translations

Despite the fact that English has become the international language of business, for multinational companies it is important to have the quality policy translated and printed for employees in all key locations around the world. This then serves as a reminder to those locations that the organization cares about them and their particular location, and sees their contribution to quality as important.

It is important to ensure that translations are done well. One company managed to catch an error before printing. They wanted to include in the graphics of the policy a catch phrase from their statement of mission, vision, and values: "Quality is in our hearts, minds and spirits." The first version of the French translation used for "spirits" a word that referred to alcoholic beverages.

Spanish is a very important language for many parts of the world, but there are many different versions of Spanish. It may be impossible to find a single wording that works well for all Spanish speakers, but enough vetting should be done to ensure that the meaning is clear to all. Similarly, it should not be assumed that Portuguese from Brazil is the same as Portuguese from Portugal.

Asian languages bring additional challenges. The prestigious *Max Planck Forschung* magazine, in an issue intended to highlight China, placed Chinese calligraphy on its cover. Only after the German-language version had been distributed did they find that the calligraphy was an advertisement for a brothel.[2] Different calligraphy was used for the international edition appearing slightly later.

The bottom line is that local staff in each country should be enlisted to review all the translations before going to print, and if possible should check the printing proofs.

## QUALITY MANUAL

The manual should be designed with all employees in mind. In the course of their daily work, employees normally see only a small fraction of the QMS so important to the company. The manual provides an opportunity to give each person a clear picture of the quality system as a whole.

The manual should be easy to read. The regulatory language of the Quality System Regulation and the "ISO-speak" of ISO 13485 and other applicable regulations and standards need to be put into plain language and terms meaningful within the company.

The organization of the manual should reflect the structure of the quality system, whether ISO, FDA, or a company-specific structure. The opportunity should be taken to provide some brief general information about the company at the start of the manual. If the ISO structure has been chosen, there are three "unused" numbers that can be used for introductory material, after which the numbering of the manual sections can correspond to the structure of ISO 13485. See Table 6.2 for an example.

**TABLE 6.2**

Example Manual Outline for Quality System with ISO 13485 Framework

1. Importance of Quality to the Business
2. Role of Manual
3. Business Information
4. Quality System Overview
5. Management Responsibility
6. Resource Management
7. Product Realization
8. Measurement, Analysis, and Improvement

---

[2] Cover, *Max Planck Forschung*, German-language edition, March 2008, reported in *The Independent*, December 2008.

If the FDA structure has been chosen, it is logical to have an introductory section, seven sections in the manual corresponding to the QSIT structure, and one section related to business considerations. See Table 6.3 for an example.

The text in the manual should cover most of the content of 21 CFR 820 and ISO 13485 but should not aim to cover every detail. For example, coverage of a special subject such as "manufacturing material" is best left to the Level 2 documentation aimed specifically at persons responsible for manufacturing areas. The goal in writing the manual should be a document short enough to be read in a single sitting—and clear and interesting enough so the reader does not fall asleep.

Some companies appear to feel the need to include all QMS requirements in the manual. Although this practice may be beneficial to external auditors and to the quality staff managing external audits, it leads to manuals that put the average employee to sleep. Documentation needs to be planned to benefit first the employees and the company; external auditors know how to adjust. Quality and regulatory staff can adjust as well.

One detail that should be included in the manual is a list of the national and international regulations and standards for the countries where the company intends to market products. This fulfills at least two important functions. It allows other procedures simply to reference the manual, rather than having lists of regulations and standards in each procedure. In addition, with an increasing number of countries imposing audit requirements on medical device companies, it is important to have evidence in the manual that attention is being given to the requirements of those countries.

**TABLE 6.3**

Example Manual Outline for Quality System with FDA QSIT Framework

1. Introduction
2. Management Controls
3. Design Controls
4. Production and Process Controls
5. Corrective and Preventive Action
6. Documents, Records, and Change Control
7. Facilities and Equipment
8. Material Controls
9. Marketing and Sales

## Look and Feel

Documentation should be managed electronically; electronic copies should be the official copies for other document levels. However, the manual should be a hard copy. The goal is to provide a copy for each employee as a tangible connection to the QMS. In this way employees can review personal copies of the manual and find their roles within the QMS. The personal copy provides employees with evidence that the company values their roles.[3]

Just as noted above for the quality policy, it is important that the manual be printed with the same quality graphics and look that are used in marketing materials. All employees are aware of the importance of marketing and sales materials. When they see a key publication for quality being given the same level of attention, they also see that the company is sincere in its attention to the QMS.

A very effective addition to the manual can be pictures of company products, processes, buildings, or employees. Pictures of products may lead to a perceived need for more frequent revision of the manual as new products come on the market. Pictures of processes need to be managed so that they do not reveal any company secrets. And there may be releases needing signature for pictures of any identifiable employees.

## External Value

Serious consideration should be given to designing the manual in a way that makes it possible for it to be a public document. Making copies available to customers can help to emphasize the value of quality for the company. If expense is a consideration, this can be done by way of PDF file on the company website.

In today's world, customers are likely to have their own QMS, with their own need for supplier assessment and qualification. A well-crafted quality manual may substantially assist the company to be qualified as a supplier. Indeed, such a quality manual may persuade a customer that there is no need to audit this company and that they should devote their audit resources elsewhere.

---

[3] If each employee is thoroughly accustomed to using an electronic tablet for daily activities, an electronic copy of the manual available on the tablet may work.

## Challenges

It must be acknowledged that there are particular challenges to be addressed when a company chooses to use hard-copy quality manuals. At the most basic level is the question of version control. Even for a small company, it is probably not worth the time and effort to control rigorously the distribution of the manual, such as by signing upon receipt of a copy. The most practical approach is to ensure that the outside cover of each version is completely different from the previous version, so that a person can tell at a glance which version is in hand. This approach should be coupled with a training session each time a new version is created. At the training session the new version should be handed out and employees should be instructed to throw out the old.[4]

Because of the expense involved it is important to plan the content so that the printed manual does not become quickly out of date. In particular, organizational details are best left out of the manual, since reorganization is a relatively frequent occurrence for any company.

With all the best planning, it is still possible to have important updates for the manual earlier than the time planned for the next version of the manual. For this reason it is prudent to have a note inside the cover or otherwise near the front of the manual to specify the possibility that there may be manual addenda posted among the electronic documentation and that the user is responsible to check regularly for updates.

Large international companies need to plan for translation of the manual into the languages of all operations that are part of the same QMS. This is a significant concern and may lead some companies to the conclusion that they should not try to export their QMS to other countries.

On the other hand, regulatory authorities around the world are increasingly expecting to find companies managing quality through a QMS. If local operations need a QMS, it is logical for the company to gain the benefits of a worldwide standardization by promulgating the manual on a worldwide basis.

Where expense is a deciding factor, consideration may be given to the creation of a simple bifold manual. An 11 × 17 sheet of card stock, when

---

[4] One company holds a raffle where the ticket for entry in the raffle is an old copy of the manual with the person's name on it.

folded in half, provides four pages of 8½ × 11 card stock. If two columns are used per page, the result is eight columns of information, which can provide a surprisingly large amount of information—enough for an entirely satisfactory manual. (The same can be accomplished using international size A3, which folded provides four pages size A4.)[5]

---

[5] I am indebted for this concept to Edward R. Tufte, who has devoted much effort to the promotion of effective ways of presenting information. See, for example, *The Visual Display of Quantitative Information*, 2nd Edition, Cheshire CT: Graphics Press, 2001.

# 7

# Level 2 Documentation

Good Level 2 documentation is absolutely essential for the long-term success of the quality management system (QMS). While the quality manual is aimed at giving a good overall look at the big picture, the Level 2 documentation is aimed at careful enunciation of the principles that govern each of the critical process areas of the company. This documentation should state in terms of basic principles what must be done, who must do it (and, in some cases, when it must be done).

One of the values of good Level 2 documentation is that it makes possible the concept that "quality is everyone's business." It places on the table the principles intended to govern each major process within the company. Each department thus can know expectations and can operate without a requirement for day to day policing by the quality/regulatory functions.

There should be no need for more than a couple of dozen Level 2 procedures. Table 7.1 provides a list of procedures that can work (corresponding to processes identified earlier), although there is nothing sacred about this particular list. The point is that it is possible to encompass the entire QMS in a modest list of basic, high-level procedures.

This list of procedures is compatible with either the FDA Framework or the ISO Framework, as noted in Chapter 3.

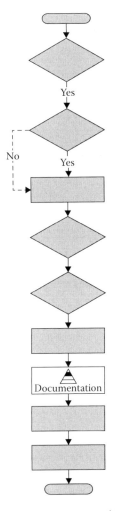

Documentation Level 2

**TABLE 7.1**

Level 2 Procedures

1. Management Responsibility
2. Risk Management
3. Documentation Management
4. Records Management
5. Internal Audits
6. Qualification and Training
7. Facilities and Equipment
8. Software and Process Validation
9. Design Control
10. Supplier Quality Management
11. Product Regulatory Compliance
12. Production
13. Inspection, Test, and Disposition
14. Handling, Storage, Preservation, and Delivery
15. Service and Support
16. Marketing and Sales
17. Change Control
18. Customer Feedback Management
19. Corrective and Preventive Action
20. Control of Nonconforming Product

## VALUE TO THE EMPLOYEE

Most employees are actively involved in only a few of the key processes in the company. Thus, there are probably only a few Level 2 procedures that directly affect their day-to-day activities and with which they need to be particularly familiar.

In day-to-day work, employees are generally swamped with their workload and mired in the details of exactly what they are expected to do. They are usually working within the details of Level 3 procedures that provide "how-to" instructions for handling the challenges of each day's work. In a real life situation not every challenge that arises is straightforward and fits clearly into categories spelled out in these procedures. In such instances, the principles enunciated in applicable Level 2 procedures can provide important insight into what is truly required and thus can guide decisions.

Most managers should have some familiarity with all of the Level 2 procedures, but will want to give particular attention to the procedures governing processes involving their departments. Although the quality organization can and must give careful attention to the content of Level 2 procedures, it is not practical to expect the quality organization to be fully aware of details in departmental procedures (Level 3). It should be the responsibility of managers to use the applicable Level 2 procedures to ensure that departmental procedures and practices are appropriately aligned with what must be done.

## THE PRINCIPLES APPLICABLE TO EACH PROCESS

The quality manual and Level 2 together should contain essentially all applicable wording from 21 CFR 820, ISO 13485, and other regulations or standards applicable to the QMS for the company. It is to be expected that there will be some duplication between the manual and the Level 2 documentation. In such instances, in the manual the emphasis should be on the readability of the subject matter. In Level 2 procedures, the emphasis must be on ensuring that all the requirements applicable to the particular process are clearly and fully expressed.

Level 2 documentation should include principles for QMS considerations that go beyond explicit requirements from standards and regulations. For example, the procedure for management responsibility is the logical home for principles establishing a quality council. The procedure for facilities and equipment should include a provision to ensure that quality and regulatory concerns are adequately addressed in capital purchases.

It may in some instances be useful to include flowcharts in Level 2 procedures. For example, in the process identified as "Customer Feedback Management" it may be useful for a flowchart to clarify the management of customer calls to ensure that:

- Potential adverse events are properly routed for evaluation and reporting.
- True complaints (meeting regulatory definitions) are identified and distinguished from other issues, such as delivery delays.
- Complaints are properly evaluated and, where appropriate, investigated.
- Any other steps needed for closure are made clear.

For international quality management systems, in order to obtain full benefit from Level 2 procedures, these procedures must be available in the languages in which they will be used. It is always advisable to keep procedures as short as possible; reducing the extent of what must be translated is a bonus for succinct procedures. A less satisfactory approach would be to require that managers be fluent in the language used for the Level 2 procedures so that they can ensure that their departmental procedures in the local language are consistent with the required principles.

---

## APPENDIX

Appendix C addresses the details of contents for the suggested list of Level 2 procedures of Table 7.1. Although not making claims for completeness, it gives an idea of the kinds of requirements that need to be in such procedures in order to fulfill requirements of 21 CFR 820 and ISO 13485, as well as the European requirements of directives and regulations. It may be a useful starting point for a company intending to establish a meaningful Level 2 structure.

# 8

## Level 3 Documentation

Level 3 procedures address the how-to details of what needs to be done. This means they deserve serious attention, particularly in those areas that are critical for patient safety and regulatory compliance.

### CORPORATION-WIDE LEVEL 3

Although most Level 3 procedures will be local procedures, in critical areas larger companies will want to ensure that key subjects are handled uniformly across the organization. And even for smaller companies these are exactly the subject areas that deserve extra attention.

#### Complaints

Uniform handling of complaints begins with the definition of the word itself. A sensible choice is to use the U.S. Food and Drug Administration (FDA) definition: "any written, electronic, or oral communication that alleges deficiencies related to the identity, quality, durability, reliability, safety, effectiveness, or performance of a device after it is released for distribution." Despite the apparent clarity and completeness of this definition, experience indicates that significant training efforts are required to ensure

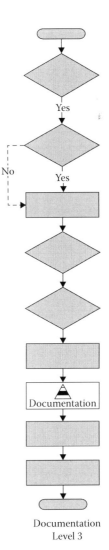

Documentation
Level 3

uniform application of the definition across many sites, especially when many countries are involved.[1]

In addition, since the complaint definition does not include issues that are business-related, such as on-time deliveries, it can be worthwhile creating a different category of "complaint" covering only business issues. This allows more flexible handling of business issues by not requiring, for business issues, all of the regulatory requirements that must be applied for complaints meeting the FDA definition.

An additional consideration relates to the nature of each complaint. Some complaints can be handled satisfactorily by the call center and support staff in the country where the call is received. In other cases, it will be necessary to escalate the concern to support facilities centrally located.

All of these considerations dictate the need for a detailed Level 3 procedure that spells out exactly how all of these complex questions are to be addressed. See Appendix D for further consideration of this subject.

## Medical Device Reporting/Vigilance

The process for addressing potential adverse events—a process intimately connected with complaint handling—is also a process where worldwide uniformity of approach is important. Of course, the details of how such issues must be handled do vary from one country or region to another. Nevertheless, regulatory authorities are routinely sharing information on such events, and a company that chooses complete local autonomy for handling of such issues is likely to receive surprise inquiries from regulatory authorities who discover inconsistent behavior.

Even in cases where a process is established to ensure a centralized review of such issues, it may rarely occur that local staff perceive their legal requirements differently from the decision arising from the central review. In such instances local staff will act in accordance with their perception of local legal requirements. That is to say, even if the centralized review determines that an event is not reportable, local staff will report it

---

[1] ISO 13485:2016 provides a more encompassing choice of definition: "written, electronic, or oral communication that alleges deficiencies related to the identity, quality, durability, reliability, usability, safety or performance of a medical device that has been released from the organization's control or related to a service that affects the performance of such medical device." Since this definition adds some complexity, its use (advisable for companies certified to the new standard) will mean more training to ensure uniform application.

to their authorities if they believe reporting is required. Thus, inconsistencies may arise on a worldwide basis. As long as good communication is maintained, these instances will not arise as unpleasant surprises. They may be unpleasant but will not be surprises.

## CAPA

The value in a consistent approach to corrective and preventive action arises from both a compliance point of view and a business point of view.

The ultimate and most unpleasant corrective action is of course a field corrective action—a recall of some sort. Clearly it is essential that such actions be carried out in a consistent manner around the world. A procedure spelling out the details required for a worldwide recall is important to have in place, while hoping it may never need to be exercised.

From the business point of view it is important to ensure that the routine aspects of corrective and preventive action are carried out consistently. If one site puts every little issue into the corrective and preventive action (CAPA) system and another site treats most issues as corrections, moving very few issues into the CAPA system, there will be major inconsistencies across the organization as a whole, and it will be difficult to assess the development of the quality management system (QMS) across the organization. A robust business-wide Level 3 CAPA procedure will promote the development of a consistent approach to quality throughout the company. If the foundation for that procedure is a software application implemented at all sites, the result will be even more beneficial.

## Quality Audits

Although it may be possible to create a single corporate-wide Level 3 procedure to cover the variety of quality audits, since these are fundamentally separate kinds of audits, it may make the most sense to have three procedures to cover three types of quality audits: external audits, supplier audits, and internal audits.

In the case of external audits, a corporate-wide Level 3 procedure is important for ensuring that auditors from regulatory authorities and other external parties are appropriately received, and that staff are aware of the importance of honest, open answers to questions asked. Moreover, there should be an established mechanism for sharing the results of each external audit throughout the organization. For example, when the FDA visits one site of a company and issues findings, they expect that when they visit another site of the same company that second site will be aware of those findings and will have taken any needed actions on those same issues at their site.

For companies selling products in Europe, notified bodies have begun the practice of conducting unannounced audits of production areas. Company procedures need to ensure that in the event of such unannounced audits, staff are aware of the needed steps to be taken, such as identification of back-up responsible persons in the event that the primary responsible person is not available.

Supplier audits involve many departments; a governing Level 3 procedure can ensure that all parties are working effectively together. And with heavy emphasis in some companies on outsourcing—to the extent that some companies are almost "virtual"—close attention to supplier quality management is critical. Supplier quality audits is where this attention to detail begins and is maintained.

Internal audits are the mechanism through which senior management and the quality organization can have a picture of how the QMS is functioning. If internal audits are not carried out in a consistent manner across all sites of the organization it will be impossible to develop such a picture. This requires a Level 3 procedure applicable across the company.

## FORMAT

Because Level 3 procedures need to cover extensive detail, it is possible for such procedures to become confusing to the people who need them the most. A couple of approaches can be used to help simplify.

### Flowcharts

There is no substitute for a good flowchart in clarifying details of what needs to be carried out in what sequence. Often, in the development of a flowchart for an existing procedure, it may be discovered that the words of the procedure are specifying sequences that ultimately make no sense. A flowchart is capable of forcing reality in the situation. Good flowcharts lead to business processes that are well understood by the people working on those processes. If related processes are all mapped with flowcharts where relationships between processes are clear, the business functions better.

On the other hand, if not well managed, flowcharts can contribute to confusion rather than alleviating it. For example:

- It is possible for the creator of a flowchart to become obsessed with the need to fit the entire flowchart on a single page. This can lead to a flowchart that causes eyes to glaze over, providing no benefit.
- Another problem can arise when the flowcharts are treated as simply attachments without a clear relationship to the wording of the procedure. The result can be words giving one message while the flowchart gives a different message. The flowchart needs to be an integral part of the procedure. Each icon on the flowchart should have a number, and that number should correspond to the same number in the text of the procedure. See Appendix D for an example.

## Playscript Procedures

Playscript procedures are procedures written essentially as the name suggests: like the script for a play. The responsible party for a given action appears in the left-hand column, and the action required appears in the right-hand column. See Appendix E for an example. This approach functions much like a flowchart without the chart. Although this can be an extremely useful approach that makes clear who is responsible for each step of action in the procedure, many individuals feel a resistance in first using procedures written in this style. With training and experience the resistance can be overcome, but some resistance appears to be natural and should be expected.

## Language

Since procedures are specifying required actions, it is essential that the people using the procedures are comfortable with the language in the procedure. If this means translation, then translation must be carried out. This is a case where the value of flowcharts, perhaps augmented by a playscript approach, may help. The more simple and visual the approach, the fewer words required.

## SOFTWARE

For many critical quality functions, software applications are available, as noted earlier. To the extent that the software guides or constrains the user, it may be possible to reduce the detail in Level 3 procedures. It may even be possible that screens appear in the appropriate language of the user.

In choosing software for these functions, as in all cases for QMS software, it is critical to decide the required functionality of the software to meet company needs, rather than purchasing a package and then trying to fit company needs into that package.

## KEEPING CURRENT

Level 3 procedures are the procedures that most employees use on a day-to-day basis. This can lead to a situation where they become so familiar that they develop the habit of working for extended periods of time without reference to the procedure. This in turn can lead to actions that are not consistent with the procedures. There is no easy solution to this problem. Internal audits can help.

Staff can be reminded from time to time that they should be checking their actions against the procedures. If they then find a discrepancy between what the Level 3 procedure says to do and what they are actually doing, they have two choices: (1) they can go back to doing what the procedure specifies, or (2) if their actions are sensible and consistent with requirements of Level 2 procedures, the Level 3 procedure can be changed to reflect the actions. (For some reason, such reminders seem to be most common at times just before announced third-party audits, but they are appropriate at other times as well.)

# 9

## Level 4 Documentation

Level 4 documentation tends to be a kind of catch-all category. Most documentation pyramids include in Level 4 the category of "Records," but beyond that there may be a variety of kinds of documents that don't fit readily into other categories but need to be controlled. There is no consensus on what needs to be in Level 4 documentation and no need for consensus. There is a logic to ensuring that all controlled documentation is included in one of the documentation levels, but no particular requirement for doing so. It is certainly possible to control a documentation category without requiring it to be an element in the documentation pyramid.

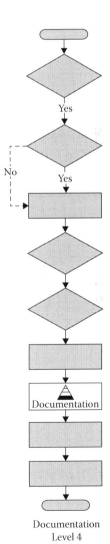

Documentation
Level 4

### RECORDS

Most companies specify that the records of fulfillment of the requirements in other procedures are considered to be in Level 4. This means quite a large number of documents. Although there is no external requirement for doing so, it is a good practice to require each manager to identify the records that are maintained by or for the manager's department. Often managers think of quality management system (QMS) records as being records for the quality department and need to be reminded of the variety of quality records.

In virtually all cases this includes some quantity of electronic records. Therefore, both regulatory and common-sense business requirements dictate the need for attention to ensuring the safety of those records.

## FORMS

Some companies choose to include "Forms" as a document category for Level 4. Others include forms as part of the documentation level for the procedures governing the forms, usually Level 3. As long as the message is clear to company employees, either way can work.

It is generally not useful to treat forms as attachments to procedures, although it may be useful to attach an example of a form that has been filled out as an attachment to a Level 3 procedure. Also, each form should be annotated in some way to make it clear to users (and, incidentally, auditors) the procedure governing the form.

It is awkward for a form to carry its own revision history; the revision history for a form is generally better kept in the procedure governing the form. Procedures are normally revised more frequently than forms, and maintaining independence of forms allows revision of the procedure without revising the form.

## GUIDELINES/GUIDANCES

Many companies, particularly large companies, find it useful to create guidelines (or guidances) for the business as a whole. These guidelines address important, but not necessarily critical, processes where there are sound business or quality reasons for encouraging (but not necessarily requiring) consistency of behavior. The company normally expects local facilities to treat these guidelines as having the same kind of authority as a U.S. Food and Drug Administration (FDA) guidance document. That is to say, local facilities are expected to follow the guideline unless there is a clear rationale for accomplishing the same thing by an alternative means.

Because such guidelines are usually implemented as substitutes for Level 3 companywide procedures, some companies choose to consider these documents as Level 3 documents. Other companies choose Level 4.

Again, as long as the message is clear to company employees, either way can work. Whether assigned to Level 3 or Level 4, in order to be truly helpful to users each guideline must clearly indicate the Level 2 procedure for which the guideline is providing implementation instructions. (If the guideline is providing instructions for a Level 3 procedure, then it should be linked to that Level 3 procedure in some manner.)

## TRAINING MATERIALS

Training modules in the form of slides, or web-based modules, together with tests to be used to demonstrate training effectiveness and any other training materials are often forgotten as documents to be controlled. This is regrettable because the need may arise to determine exactly what was covered in a training session. There may be clear documentation of who attended and what the title of the session was and rather fuzzy information about what was covered. Often the only information is found on someone's personal computer. This is not a reliable means for controlling documentation.

This documentation deserves the same level of attention as other documents, including some practical level of control of approvals and changes.

## EXTERNAL DOCUMENTATION

There are a large number of external documents of importance to each company. Some examples are likely to be applicable:

- QMS regulations worldwide
- Regulatory guidelines
- QMS standards
- Regulations for product approval to market in all countries where the company expects to market products
- Product-related standards

All of these documents must be identified in order for the company to place its products in the various markets. However, if the right documents are not identified in a timely manner, product introductions may be delayed unnecessarily, with resulting effect on the bottom line. For example, late discovery of a new product registration requirement in a particular country may mean late marketing of the product in that country.

Depending on the type of product offered by the company, the last category on the list, product-related standards, may be the most difficult to manage. Not only must all the applicable standards be identified, but also a system must be implemented to ensure that the most current versions of these standards are available for use to the persons ensuring conformance to those standards. This is important not only for product development (where current standards must be applied), but also after the product is on the market: Revisions to a standard applied to a product on the market must be assessed to evaluate implications for that product.

Once the applicable external documents have been identified, various resources can be used to keep the information up to date.

- Some regulatory authorities provide an email service that sends update information on a regular basis. The FDA is the most important of these.
- The Regulatory Affairs Professional Society provides members with updates on regulatory information worldwide.
- Online searches will identify consultant organizations that provide regulatory updates on requirements for marketing around the world.
- Some service providers monitor changes in product standards and send notifications of updates.

Each company must decide the most effective means for controlling the external documentation and for making these documents readily available to those in the company that needs them.

# 10

## *Fully Incorporating Risk Management*

Risk management is a subject that has received a lot of attention in recent years. Risk management is important to each business in terms of managing all risks related to the business.[1,2] Indeed, there is an international standard for risk management: ISO 31000:2009.[3] Principles of risk management are critical for patient safety in healthcare organizations.[4]

Concern for patient safety drives medical device companies to focus particularly on product and process risk management. The key standard is ISO 14971, recently updated with annexes to provide additional information beyond the text (which remains identical to the 2007 publication) with regard to European requirements.[5] A guidance for application has been published.[6] An excellent guide is also available from the Canadian Standards Association.[7] A book has been published recently addressing risk management for healthcare products.[8]

The Quality System Regulation includes the word "risk" only once, in 820.30(g): "Design validation shall include software validation and risk analysis, where appropriate." More importantly, it is clear from recent

---

[1] Peter L. Bernstein, *Against the Gods: The Remarkable Story of Risk*, New York: Wiley, 1998.

[2] John Fraser and Betty J. Simkins, eds., *Enterprise Risk Management*, New York: Wiley, 2010.

[3] BS ISO 31000:2009, Risk management: Principles and guidelines.

[4] Barbara J. Youngberg, ed., *Principles of Risk Management and Patient Safety*, Sudbury, MA: Jones & Bartlett Learning, 2011.

[5] BS EN ISO 14971:2012 Medical devices: Application of risk management to medical devices (ISO 14971:2007, Corrected version 2007-10-01).

[6] ISO/TR 24971:2013, Medical devices—Guidance on the application of ISO 14971.

[7] PLUS 14971, *The ISO 14971:2007 Essentials: A Practical Handbook for Implementing the ISO 14971 Standard for Medical Devices*, Canadian Standards Association, Mississauga, Ontario, Canada, 2007.

[8] Edwin Bills and Stan Mastrangolo, eds., *Lifecycle Risk Management for Healthcare Products*, River Grove, IL, DHI Publishing, 2016.

guidance documents[9] that the U.S. Food and Drug Administration (FDA) expects companies to be implementing risk management principles throughout their organization. Risk management is becoming essential to how the FDA does business, and the FDA expects the same from medical device manufacturers.

Guidance on incorporation of risk management principles into a QMS has been available for many years.[10] ISO 13485:2016 incorporates many aspects of this guidance.[11] This is one of the best qualities of the 2016 revision.

## QUALITY MANUAL

The quality manual should make clear the importance of product risk management throughout the QMS. This should be made clear in general terms, but in addition, the specific application of risk management principles should be addressed from design through supplier quality management, production processes, and post-market activities.

## LEVEL 2

Risk management principles must be incorporated throughout Level 2 procedures. Nevertheless, it is useful to have a separate Level 2 procedure devoted specifically to product risk management. Such a procedure should focus particularly on the responsibilities of top management as defined in ISO 14971:

---

[9] Examples:
  - CDRH, "Guidance for Industry and Food and Drug Administration Staff: Factors to Consider When Making Benefit-Risk Determinations in Medical Device Premarket Approval and *De Novo* Classifications," March 28, 2012.
  - CDRH, "Oversight of Clinical Investigations: A Risk-Based Approach to Monitoring," August 2013.

[10] GHTF/SG3/N15R8, "Implementation of Risk Management Principles and Activities with a Quality Management System," Global Harmonization Task Force Study Group 3, 2005, now available through the International Medical Device Regulators Forum at www.imdrf.org under "Documents."

[11] ISO 13485:2016, Medical Devices: Quality Management Systems: Requirements for Regulatory Purposes.

- Definition of a policy for determining acceptability criteria for risks
- Review of the suitability of the company's risk management processes (normally as part of the management review process)
- Ensuring that adequate resources are available for risk management
- Ensuring that employees assigned to risk management tasks are qualified

To complement the Level 2 procedure on risk management that provides an overview, risk management principles should be spelled out in many other Level 2 procedures.[12]

- In design control it is clear that risk management principles must be an integral part of the process, from conception through the development of production processes.
- In supplier quality management, assessment of risks should determine the extent of the supplier evaluation required, both initially and on an ongoing basis. Risk management must receive particular emphasis in any outsourcing of processes.
- The extent of required validation, both process validation and software validation, should be determined on the basis of the risks involved.
- The extent of incoming inspection should be influenced by the assessment of the supplier and the risks associated with the material supplied.
- In change control, assessment of risks associated with the change must be a part of the process, including explicit reference to use of the risk management file.
- In training, the extent of the effectiveness check should be determined on the basis of the risks involved if the subject of the training is performed incorrectly.
- Feedback from customers must be used to update risk management files when needed.

The need for a risk-based approach is implied in other areas.

---

[12] For additional detail, see Appendix C.

- Risk management must be considered in the choice of any software used for QMS infrastructure both as to risks involved with the software itself, as well as whether the software facilitates risk management considerations related to the subject matter of the software.
- Product inspections at all stages of production should be based on determination of the risks involved. In-process inspection should be influenced by the evaluation of process risks. Final inspection must be able to verify critical performance characteristics.
- In control of nonconforming product, assessment of risks should play a key role in disposition decisions. A decision to rework must be based on confidence that the rework process will not introduce new risks. Assessment of potential risks to patients plays a critical role in determining the need for field corrective actions when product has already been delivered.
- In corrective and preventive action, risk management principles should be part of the criteria for determining the extent of attention needed for the various issues that arise.
- With regard to internal audits, a risk-based approach should be used both in planning the audits and in assessing the importance of findings.
- Postproduction, risk management principles need to be applied in handling of complaints and in assessing adverse events.

Particular attention must be given to ensuring that risk management information about a product is consistent from conception to delivery. When a product is on the market and becomes involved in an adverse event, the regulatory staff, often with advice from a medical officer or medical consultant, must determine the level of risk to the patient in the situation. In the ideal case, persons involved in assessment of the adverse event will be able to turn to the risk management file, which will have already considered the possibility of this kind of event and will provide the needed background for decisions.

However, if the risk management file did not address this kind of event, or if the persons carrying out the assessment of the adverse event determine the level of risk differently from what the assessment was in the design process, this can be a source of serious problems. All players, including medical advisors, must be involved in the product risk management process from start to finish in order to assure well-being to patients (and the company).

## LEVEL 3

It is widely recognized that risk management principles must be fully incorporated into detailed procedures for design control.

There are several aspects of dealing with issues postproduction where risk management principles need to be incorporated into the "how-to" of various required actions:

- The risk management file provides guidance on which reporting deadline applies to a particular event. For example, it helps to assess whether the event represents an immediate threat to public health. Such a situation in most jurisdictions has a very short reporting time requirement, and the risk management file facilitates a quick decision.
- The risk management file assists with preparing a Health Hazard Analysis for Medical Device Reporting in the United States.
- Complaint records must be analyzed to ensure that observed problems are consistent with information in the risk management file. If new hazards are identified, the risk management file must be updated.
- In the case of in vitro diagnostics (IVDs), there can arise changes in the pathogen or markers that affect test performance; this will also require changes in the risk management file.
- In extreme cases, it can happen that a risk previously identified as acceptable would become unacceptable. This would mean serious consequences for the product.[13]
- Periodic assessments based on post-market surveillance should be carried out to verify that products continue to meet "state-of-the-art" requirements for product safety that are explicit in some jurisdictions and implicit in others.

As a general rule, it is prudent for managers and other employees to consider each process for the role that product risk management should play in that process, and then take steps to ensure that those principles are fully implemented in the process.

---

[13] For example, some years ago it was considered a positive feature that blood glucose meters could be set by the customer to the desired unit of measure, mg/dL or mmol/L. One company had an issue leading to adverse events (unintentional switching from mg/dL to mmol/L). The eventual upshot was that all companies manufacturing blood glucose meters were expected almost overnight to treat this previously "positive" feature as an unacceptable risk.

# 11

## Implementation

Although "implementation" is indicated as simply one block on the flowchart, the concept has many facets. Most of these will be specific to each company. However, there are some aspects of implementation that are important for all companies.

## COMMUNICATION

The single most important aspect of implementation is communication with all who are affected by the changes. Of course there is a requirement in ISO 13485 that communication should take place regarding the effectiveness of the QMS. However, the communication is more important than simply fulfilling a requirement. In fact, the success of the quality plan to put in place a QMS for benefit of patients and the company depends on good communication throughout the plan implementation. Every available communication vehicle should be used: informative emails and text messages, postings on bulletin boards and internal websites, newsletters, general meetings, and more.

It is almost impossible to have too many vehicles of communication because, if we are completely honest with ourselves, we must acknowledge that probably 90% of these communications will be ignored. That is only natural. People are busy with their own responsibilities. We must work with the situation,

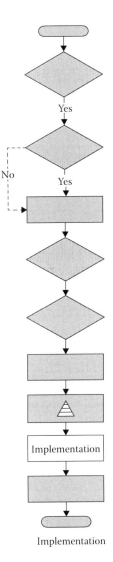

Implementation

and the best way to do this is not by berating our colleagues for inattention, but by patiently repeating the message.

We need to take advantage particularly when we have items that can be distributed, such as personal copies of the quality policy and the quality manual. Rather than simply sending out these items in the interoffice mail, we should hand these items out personally at meetings. The meetings can be either meetings called for this specific purpose (and to cover some significant aspect of the QMS implementation) or this material can be added to meetings already scheduled, either general or departmental.

The implementation of the new procedures and infrastructure should in all cases be foreshadowed by communications that say what is coming and why. Remember that the documentation pyramid accounts for the what, the who, and the how. There is no why. As noted earlier, it is not appropriate in procedures themselves to explain in detail why a particular procedure is needed. In some cases the why is obvious. However, this may not be apparent. People become more willing participants if they know why they are doing what they are doing. It is in the communication (and, of course, the training) related to the elements of the QMS that people can learn the why.

---

## RESOURCES

### Human Resources

The steering committee/quality council and QMS support staff should be established at the start of the implementation process. Ideally, the support staff will prepare the quality plan for review by the steering committee/ quality council before it goes for approval by senior management. The support staff can then monitor and guide progress in implementation on a day-to-day basis, with at least monthly oversight by the committee/council.

### Infrastructure

As noted earlier, there are many good software applications available to support quality management systems. The plan identifies those that can be implemented in the time frame for establishment of the new QMS. It is important to ensure that these applications are validated before they go live. Well-validated systems that do what they are supposed to do lead to contented users, who find this an encouragement in their lives. This in turn leads them to be more positive about further QMS enhancements down the road.

## DOCUMENTATION

Documentation does not write itself. And although there are some sources of generic documentation which can be helpful (including Appendix C of this book), even with generic documentation as a starting point, the documentation must be tailored for the company and its QMS. What is the best approach?

In the ideal case, a lead manager will be identified to be responsible for each of the identified key processes. This person will know from the start that he or she will be the person sitting across from the external auditor to respond to questions about the process and thus should lead the development of the appropriate procedures governing that process. At the same time it should be acknowledged that not all managers comfortable at leading a process are also comfortable with writing procedures. It is important that at least one person on the QMS support staff be comfortable preparing procedures, which can then be reviewed by the lead manager for the process and others as appropriate. An alternative approach would be to engage external resources for the bolus of work involved in drafting procedures for the initial push.

## TRAINING

Training is a critical component of the QMS implementation. Some training subjects are general:

- A new or modified quality policy. (In fact, even if the quality policy is not changing, there may be value in reviewing the current policy to provide the opportunity for all to be educated again on its importance.[1])
- The manual. This is a prime opportunity for giving all an overview of the QMS.

Training for these subjects will be most effective live, providing an opportunity for the exchange of ideas. And of course a live person is (almost always) more engaging than a computer screen.

---

[1] There is no way to be certain that all are getting the message. An employee at one company was observed telling an external auditor that he was unfamiliar with the quality policy despite the fact that he had been to a training session the week before that covered the subject, and a copy of the policy was posted on the wall behind the employee as he was facing the auditor.

As each new or revised procedure is ready for implementation, training should be carried out prior to the implementation date. This can be done in live sessions or can be done online.

Online training has some advantages. Each person can carry out the training at a convenient time, rather than being obliged to schedule work around training sessions. If the online system has been well designed, the effectiveness check for the training can be administered electronically, and the results recorded in the employee's training record. For a large company with multiple sites, online training can ensure that each employee receives the same quality of training. On balance, online training provides many benefits, but it should not be used as the sole approach. Some personal contact is necessary lest the QMS become in the minds of employees a kind of impersonal robot.

Training on procedures may uncover hidden issues within the quality system. As employees are trained and retrained on procedures for which they are responsible, they may identify instances where procedures are duplicating subject matter. In some cases, the procedures may even be contradictory in what they are saying should be done. This provides an opportunity for elimination of procedures not needed.

# 12

## Maintenance (and Improvement)

Aristotle taught that moral virtue comes about as a result of habit.[1] So also by developing the right habits, we are best able to maintain our QMS. In fact, through the habits we cultivate, we will be able not only to maintain it, but to improve it as well.

Regulations and quality standards for medical device companies would have us believe that "maintenance" is the watchword. Officially, this is correct. One of the reasons to justify the original establishment of ISO 13485 as a stand-alone standard was the requirement in ISO 9001:2000 for continual improvement of the QMS—a requirement deemed inappropriate in a regulated industry. Although in regulations the authorities do not in so many words require improvements to quality management systems, in fact when investigators/auditors come to inspect, the expectations seem greater with each succeeding visit. This can create awkward situations, but on balance it is positive. Without a doubt, we should be improving our QMS—if not for regulatory, then for competitive reasons.

## METRICS

For each QMS process ISO 13485 requires figuring out a way to determine if the process is effective,

Yes

No    Yes

Maintenance

No end

Maintenance

---

[1] Aristotle, *Nicomachean Ethics*, II:1, 1103a, Revised Edition, London: Penguin Books, 2004.

monitoring the process, and taking action if necessary to maintain effectiveness. This basically means establishing at least one metric for each process. As noted in Chapter 6, metrics should also be in place to be able to determine the extent to which statements in the quality policy are being achieved.

Metrics may be established in a straightforward way for most processes. Indeed, even without a QMS requirement, most managers are already measuring something in their processes to determine their success level and to determine when they may need to intervene if the process is going poorly. Nevertheless, metrics are not always as straightforward as they seem, and attention should be given to some concerns.

- We need to be wary of unintended consequences of a metric. A classic example is known as the "cobra effect." Many years ago, British imperial authorities in India wanted to reduce the cobra population in Delhi, so they offered a reward for each dead cobra. As they should probably have anticipated, this practice led to an increase in the cobra population because people began raising cobras to be able to collect the reward.[2]

  In a situation more likely within a QMS, a simple count of negative items is often not useful as a metric because the metric can be made to improve by ignoring or not reporting some of those negative items.

- We need to have some confidence that a metric is really measuring what we think it is measuring. A good metric for new product development might seem be to determine the number of product improvements that were initiated in the first year after a product's introduction; higher numbers might indicate a defective product development process and lower numbers might indicate a good product development process. However, an astute observer in one company noted that as far as he could see the number of product improvement projects in the first year after product introduction was a straightforward function of the number of staff available to work on product improvements.

---

[2] Charley Morrow, Managing with Metrics: Watch Out for Unintended Consequences, *Leadership Insights Blog*, Linkage.com, May 30, 2014.

- We should seek, where possible, to identify "upstream" rather than "downstream" measurements. Because of the large expenses involved, it is natural for a company to count the number of field corrective actions as one of its metrics. However, this is a downstream measurement; the adverse consequences have already arrived. More useful to the company will be a metric that occurs earlier in the process, such as a measurement of material or intermediate product release; monitoring such a metric might allow intervention to avert the disaster of a correction in the field. Unfortunately, it is often quite challenging to identify a meaningful upstream metric.
- We should seek to make the collection of metrics consume as little time as possible. When the collection of information about processes begins to take many hours, or even days, of a person's time, people rightly begin to question the value.
- We need to ensure that someone is reviewing the metrics after they are collected. The whole intent behind the metrics is not to have something to show to auditors, but rather to ensure that processes stay on track and even improve. If tracking a metric shows that a process is deteriorating, some intervention to get the process back into a state of effectiveness is needed.
- This brings us to the last point. Metrics need to be timely. Tracking a production value by checking it every six months will not be useful to the business. Metrics need to be available within the time frame when intervention can be useful to get the process back on track.

Ultimately, perhaps the most important aspect of metrics is how they are used. In this, the attitude of senior management will determine whether metrics are successfully used to improve the business—or whether they turn into a game. It is imperative that metrics be used to identify and fix problems rather than being used as a means for inflicting blame and punishment on persons and groups whose metrics have deteriorated.

## INTERNAL AUDITS

Internal audits can be the most critical component in maintaining and improving the QMS. Just as metrics must not be used for punishment, so also internal audits must be carried out in a spirit of working together to uncover issues that allow improvements to be made. And they must be perceived in this manner by auditees if the process is to be fully effective.

## Many or Few Auditors?

In setting up internal audits, we need to decide whether we want to have a large number of auditors from many departments who each carry out a small number of audits each year or a small number of specialized auditors, probably in the quality department, for whom auditing is a major part of their workload. There are points for consideration:

- Using many auditors from a variety of departments emphasizes the concept that "quality is everyone's business."
- These auditors become quality ambassadors in their departments.
- New employees in any department may benefit from the opportunity (after appropriate training) to participate in internal audits with a more experienced auditor as a way to learn about how the company operates. This brings a fresh set of eyes to bear on various subjects, but it is also possible that this will be of more value to the new employee than to the company.
- When auditors come from the quality department only, it is easy for auditees to get the feeling that quality is acting like a policeman. When auditees know that auditors may come from any department, it may facilitate fewer adversarial situations.
- Auditors from other than quality or regulatory departments may find that their managers do not give them credit and reward for the time they spend as auditors. These managers may even begrudge the time allocated to audits. For this reason, in order for such a program to work, it must have senior management support and auditors must have auditing as part of their annual objectives.
- Auditor training becomes an extra challenge (and expense) when there are many auditors and each auditor only carries out one or two audits per year. The auditors may feel the need for bolstering their confidence, which can lead to significant extra time for auditors in the preparation and writing up of results.
- With a small number of auditors carrying out many more audits it should be possible for those auditors to hone skills over time so that even coming from the quality department, they may be able to

promote the idea that they are not there as police officers but rather are interested in working with the auditee to make the system better.

- With a small number of auditors it is easier to ensure that changes to address new issues in the audits can be implemented more quickly. With the increase in number of regulatory authorities interested to see that the QMS is addressing their particular interests, this becomes increasingly important.

On balance, it is probably best to work with a small group of well-trained auditors, but there are some companies that will benefit from using a large number of auditors from various departments.

## Effectiveness

Metrics to indicate effectiveness of internal audits are particularly challenging.

One metric that is bound to fail is to count the total number of nonconformities. Human nature can have an unintentional effect on outcomes. If the goal is to have the number as large as possible, internal auditors may find themselves digging a little deeper so as to get a large number. If the goal is to have the number gradually go down over a period of years, there can be an unwitting tendency to look less deeply over that time.

This type of metric might be made usable if it is possible to link audit results to financial consequences. This has the advantage of putting the findings in the language of management. On the other hand, this requires a well-implemented system for quality costs that has been validated by the finance department. Financial figures coming from quality or regulatory departments are not accorded the same authority as figures coming from finance.

In one company,[3] a metric was used for a while that was created by a manager who came from an accounting background. This took the total number of internal audit nonconformities divided by the total of both external audit and internal audit nonconformities times 100 to give a metric as a percentage. The results were plausible, and behavioral tendencies did not appear to result in manipulation of the results. On the other hand, the metric itself was confusing to many, and ultimately it was concluded that the results were too positive.

---

[3] Personal experience, Bayer Diagnostics.

A more promising approach may be to take the position that any external finding should already have an entry in the corrective and preventive action (CAPA) system if internal audits are functioning effectively.[4] If there is an external finding that is not already being handled in the CAPA system (probably the result of an internal audit), this represents a failure of the internal audit process. The metric then is simply the number of external findings not already in CAPA, and the goal is zero. It may be appropriate to add in a multiplicative risk factor based on the seriousness of the issue.

## QUALITY COUNCIL

A quality council meeting monthly is extremely valuable to maintaining the QMS and guiding its improvement. This is the group that should be monitoring the metrics for key QMS processes. Where a metric indicates a problem, this group can initiate action in response. More importantly, where a metric indicates a potential problem, this group can identify the needed improvements as preventive actions. This is the group that should plan QMS improvements that go beyond the original quality plan to put the QMS in place. In particular, software applications that carry the company forward to the vision of what is ultimately desired should be implemented under the oversight of this group.

In large companies, this group can oversee the establishment of multisite committees to meet regularly (by teleconference or other remote conferencing method) to facilitate consistent processes across sites. If the company has decided to ensure consistent practices by implementing a Level 3 procedure for a key process, then that process is a logical subject for a multisite team. That team should then assume ownership of the Level 3 procedure. Benefits from this kind of approach can be seen in many areas.

- Consistent handling of complaints and adverse event reporting is critical for business success, since regulatory authorities around the world are comparing what they see reported.
- Comparison of internal audit findings across sites is possible only if internal audits are being administered similarly in those sites.

---

[4] This should be a recent CAPA entry. An old CAPA entry would simply provide evidence of awareness of the issue and lack of interest in solving the problem.

- If sites are using different criteria for entering issues into the CAPA system, inappropriate allocation of resources—too many or too few—can be the result at some sites.
- Process validation inconsistencies may lead either to unexpected external findings at one site or unreasonably large resources devoted to validation at another.

From time to time it is useful for the quality council to hold a review of a key component of the QMS. For example, it may be useful for the quality council to have a design review of the documentation system. This would consider what the features of the documentation system are intended to be and whether it is actually fulfilling the objectives for it.

One of the most important roles for the quality council should be oversight of the material to be presented for management review. Senior management do not have time to plow through vast reams of data about the QMS. Time available for management review is precious and should be well focused in areas where management decisions and support are needed.

Note that all of what has been discussed as responsibilities under the quality council can be carried out by the quality and/or regulatory departments. Indeed, it may even appear to be handled more quickly within those functions. However, an approach that uses quality councils, with members representing all departments, will demonstrate company-wide ownership of the QMS and will in the end prove more effective.

## MANAGEMENT REVIEW

Management review is the ultimate means for ensuring the ongoing effectiveness of the QMS. Reviews should not be more frequent than quarterly because if they are too frequent, there is a loss of perspective that can defeat the purpose of the reviews.

Often it is assumed that the senior management team, as recipients of reports from across the company, are the most well informed of all in the company. This may not be a correct assumption. Often, as reports are filtered up to the top, each succeeding manager puts a more positive spin on the information, so that by the time it reaches the top, it looks either positive or bland.

This situation places a premium on the metrics. This is the reason why it is so important to design metrics that measure what is important in the QMS processes. Good data allow the discussion to focus on what the problem is rather than who is to blame.

There is a lot of material that must be covered for management review.[5] It is essential to avoid simply throwing all the data at senior management and hoping for the best. We have to look beyond the requirements and take steps to ensure that the review is really meaningful.

In most companies, metrics will indicate most processes in good order, a few needing improvement, and perhaps even one or two needing immediate attention. The material should be handled with a stoplight approach in the material provided to reviewers ahead of the meeting. Senior managers are normally very hard working and put in long hours. For this reason, they are particularly sensitive to having their time wasted and appreciate having the material presented in a fully organized manner.

- A green light should be assigned to the processes in good order. These data can be collected in a separate section to be covered in the review only by exception. If a reviewer wishes to discuss one of these topics, it will be reviewed. Otherwise it will not be covered in the meeting.
- A yellow light should be assigned to the items needing improvement, and a red light should indicate any items that need urgent attention. These are the items that should be on the agenda for discussion. These should have a clear problem statement from the quality council as well as options for action and recommendations.

This kind of approach will lead to productive, not boring, management reviews, and will be appreciated by the senior managers, as well as the quality and regulatory functions.

## WORKING WITH REGISTRARS/NOTIFIED BODIES

In striving to maintain and improve the QMS, if the QMS is registered, we can utilize the registrar as a kind of arm's-length partner in the effort.

---

[5] See Appendix C, Management Responsibility.

## Definitions

Prior to any discussion of the subject of working with registrars or notified bodies it is important to have a clear idea of these terms. Stated briefly, a registrar assesses quality systems; a notified body assesses products.

A registrar may also be called a "certification body" or "registration body." A registrar is an organization that meets the requirements of an accreditation body and is therefore authorized to evaluate quality management systems against ISO standard requirements. In order for a QMS to have an ISO 13485 certificate, the QMS must pass an audit executed by auditors from a registrar.

A closely related function is that of notified body. A notified body is an organization nominated by a member of government and notified by the European Commission. A notified body is nominated based on specified requirements, such as knowledge, experience, independence, and resources to conduct conformity assessments. The primary role of a notified body is to provide services for conformity assessment of products in support of CE Marking in Europe. This normally means assessing the conformity of the manufacturer's products to the essential requirements listed in device directives and regulations.

For the sake of simplifying the audit process, many companies choose to have these two functions carried out by the same organization. This is possible so long as the organization has been authorized to evaluate the specific types of products produced by those companies. European authorities are currently taking steps to ensure that notified bodies are well qualified for the products they are evaluating. This effort is having the effect of reducing the number of notified bodies authorized for various classes of products. A consequence will be an increase in instances where the notified body for some of a company's products may be different from that company's registrar. This is less desirable, but completely workable.

## Relationships

The relationship of a company with its registrar, while not straightforward and simple, nevertheless should be a positive relationship. The registrar has a responsibility to ensure that the company is fulfilling the requirements of the ISO standard. It has accreditation bodies looking over its shoulder to ensure that it is properly enforcing the requirements of the standard. At the same time, the company is itself paying for the evaluation, and has, at least theoretically, the freedom to move the business to a different registrar if dissatisfied.

That relationship is further complicated when the same organization is also the notified body to evaluate products sold in Europe. In this situation, the notified body has the various regulatory authorities in Europe looking over its shoulder to ensure that the requirements of the directives and regulations are being properly applied. Notified bodies are even required to make unannounced visits to audit. Although it is possible for companies to change notified bodies, this can be significantly more difficult and expensive than a change in registrars. In many cases a change in notified body will require a change in product labeling, which is both time-consuming and expensive.

Nevertheless, many companies and registrars/notified bodies have developed productive working relationships and this should be the expectation.

## Value

Before the registrar/notified body begins to provide its services, that organization must be evaluated in the same manner as any other service provider for the QMS. In the course of the evaluation, the company needs to gain some understanding of the way in which the registrar works. Within the overall framework that requires fulfillment of all QMS requirements, there is some flexibility in the philosophy of approach. The company needs to ensure that the approach of the registrar will be congruent with company philosophy on the QMS. For example, if company philosophy is strongly oriented toward using the QMS as an important tool for business improvement, it may be worthwhile choosing as a registrar an organization that also emphasizes a desire to promote business improvement.

Registrars must be independent and therefore are not permitted to provide consulting services. Nevertheless, they are permitted to clarify requirements and companies should not hesitate to ask questions aimed at better understanding of specific requirements.

At the closing meeting of each audit, in addition to reviewing the audit report, the company can maximize value from the audit by seeking more informal observations by the auditor. This is a unique opportunity for gaining insight through the eyes of a knowledgeable person from outside the company.

At least yearly there should also be a report flowing in the other direction. Did the auditors fulfill company expectations? Were the issues raised nitpicking issues or items of serious concern? Did the administrative staff send the certificate in a timely manner? Was the certificate worded correctly? The registrar normally has its own QMS in place and is expected to deal with issues raised as complaints and possible entries in its own CAPA system.

Through this frank exchange of information, a productive relationship can be developed that provides ongoing support for the QMS.

## Multiple Sites

For a company with multiple sites, and particularly when those sites are organized as a single QMS, the registrar can provide special value. One registrar provides a common vision. Ideally, for a multisite QMS, the lead auditor should visit all sites in order to have a clear picture of all the pieces of the company and how they fit together. In such a situation, the company should expect a summary assessment across the whole QMS in addition to the formal audit reports at the close of the audit at each site.

The annual round of audits by the registrar presents a further opportunity for QMS maintenance and improvement. A person from the QMS support group should be physically present to observe all audits. This person may be able to answer questions related to the corporate perspective of the QMS, but the primary role should be observation. This person should then have the responsibility to share observations of issues—particularly intersite issues—as well as "best practices" that should be replicated at other sites across the business.

There may be legitimate reasons—historical, political, or other—for having a single QMS with different registrars and certifications at different sites. A single, unified QMS is more important than a single certificate, so there may be instances where a company must use a combination of registrars to obtain certification of the parts of the QMS. In such instances, it is even more important to ensure that a single person from the QMS support group accompanies audits at all sites so that at least one person in the organization has a picture of the entire QMS. This person will also be in a position to evaluate the approaches of the various registrars and lead in guiding registrars to fulfill the company vision of what is needed.

The audit process carried out by registrars against the requirements of ISO 13485, because of its regularity and predictable frequency (except for the unannounced visits by notified bodies), can bring a unique value to the QMS. Companies should strive to work with their registrars to maximize this value. Because of the quirky relationship described above, some may consider the term "partnership" too strong as the goal for companies in working with their registrars. Yet considering the fact that a productive relationship brings value to the company, its customers and to patients affected by their products, this may be exactly the right term.

## DEVELOPMENTS TO WATCH

Although the leaders and staff at the FDA recognize the limitations imposed on them by existing regulations, they also believe that by working together with patients, providers, and industry, they can more effectively promote the availability of safe and effective medical device products in the marketplace through a "case for quality" initiative. In 2011 the FDA issued a report that summarized issues with medical device products and proposed opportunities for improvement.[6] And in the Strategic Priorities for 2016–2017, one of the priorities was to "Promote a Culture of Quality and Organizational Excellence."[7] The latest Strategic Priorities for 2018–2020 continue to focus on these initiatives.[8]

In 2014 the FDA provided a grant to the Medical Device Innovation Consortium (MDIC) to pursue the case for quality as a joint effort among the FDA, the medical technology industry, and other key stakeholders, such as healthcare providers and patients. All the MDIC efforts deserve attention (www.mdic.org), but of particular interest for QMS improvements are two components of these efforts: a capability maturity model and a metrics initiative.

A capability maturity model should be able to provide a company with a way to assess the level at which the company's QMS is functioning, from Level 1 where processes are unpredictable, poorly controlled, and reactive, to Level 5, where there is a focus on process improvement.[9] The intent is that the QMS maturity model for medical devices should be lean and efficient and should be appropriate for companies of various size and complexity. This assessment tool, once developed, should be of interest to all companies.

The medical device metrics initiative originated as a joint program between the FDA and Xavier Health. It has now been incorporated into

---

[6] U.S. FDA, "Understanding Barriers to Medical Device Quality," October 31, 2011.
[7] U.S. FDA, "2016–2017 Strategic Priorities, Center for Devices and Radiological Health."
[8] U.S. FDA, "2018–2020 Strategic Priorities, Center for Devices and Radiological Health."
[9] Medical Device Innovation Consortium, "Maturity Model Research Report," June 2015.

the MDIC effort. Currently the focus is to identify one meaningful metric for each of three phases of the product lifecycle: preproduction, production, and postproduction. All companies should also monitor this initiative in the expectation that the metrics developed will likely be worth implementing.

The IMDRF website should also be monitored for developments. In particular, as noted above in Chapter 5, the Medical Device Single Audit Program (MDSAP) will only increase in importance in coming years. Any company wishing to sell products in Canada must heed the plans for this program.[10] And, in general, the program is likely to have important implications for a company wanting to sell products anywhere outside the United States.

And as noted earlier, recent developments in Europe have implications for QMS requirements. The new European medical device and IVD regulations and their ramifications were discussed earlier, as was the departure of the United Kingdom from the European Union (Chapter 1). Planning for these changes will ensure ongoing ability to meet requirements.

Most interesting of all recent developments was a disclosure by an FDA spokeswoman that the FDA is considering adding clauses from ISO 13485:2016 to appropriate medical device regulatory requirements.[11] The spokeswoman also said, however, that she was unable to speculate on timing.

## NEVER-ENDING STORY

Companies expand and (sometimes) shrink. Companies make acquisitions and divestments. Regulations around the world change. Standards are revised.

The QMS must be resilient. It must change to meet business needs. As long as we keep in mind the goal—good products for customers—we can ensure that the QMS will meet all the challenges of a changing world.

---

[10] Health Canada requires manufacturers to be compliant with the MDSAP program by January 1, 2019. It is clear that Health Canada is monitoring the situation and has responded to concerns expressed by small manufacturers by reducing the audit times required for small manufacturers. Manufacturers should check with their registrars for the latest information.

[11] Zachary Brennan, "FDA Considers Shift on Device Quality System Regulations," *Regulatory Focus*, online journal for Regulatory Affairs Professionals Society, 27 February 2018.

# Appendix A: Pharmaceutical Quality System Models

In 2009 the International Conference on Harmonization (ICH) published a guidance with recommendations for a Pharmaceutical Quality System (PQS).[1] The U.S. Food and Drug Administration (FDA) had earlier published a similar set of guidelines with more detail related to U.S drug regulations.[2] These guidance documents are quite helpful. Although drug regulations do not require establishment of a QMS, responsible pharmaceutical manufacturers have implemented systems tailored to their needs.

## ICH MODEL

The International Council for Harmonization of Technical Requirements for Pharmaceuticals for Human Use (ICH) Q10 guidance is probably the more influential. Figure A.1 indicates the concepts of the ICH model. Product lifecycle involves four stages:

- Pharmaceutical development
- Technology transfer
- Commercial manufacturing
- Product discontinuation

Good Management Practice (GMP) regulations in place for countries and regions encompass the last three stages as well as investigational products. Other concepts important to the Performance, Quality and Safety (PQS) embrace all four stages. The concept of management responsibility is broader in this guidance than might be expected from a medical

---

[1] International Conference on Harmonization of Technical Requirements for Pharmaceuticals for Human Use (ICH), "Guidance for Industry: Q10 Pharmaceutical Quality System," April 2009, endorsed also by FDA Center for Drug Evaluation and Research (CDER) and Center for Biologics Evaluation and Research (CBER).

[2] FDA, *Guidance for Industry: Quality Systems Approach to Pharmaceutical CGMP Regulations*, September 2006.

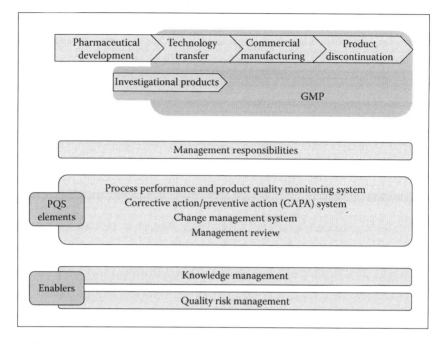

**FIGURE A.1**
ICH Q10 Pharmaceutical Quality System. (Figure Copyright International Conference on Harmonization of Technical Requirements for Pharmaceuticals for Human Use [ICH].)

device perspective. In addition to including the key factors identified in ISO 13485, such as commitment, quality policy, planning, communication, review and resources, ICH Q10 identifies management of outsourced activities and purchased materials as being under management responsibility. One additional item addressed explicitly as an item of management responsibility under this guidance is "change in product ownership"—a subject on which standards and regulations pertaining to medical devices are silent.

The model describes four elements of a PQS:

1. Process performance and product quality monitoring system
2. Corrective action and preventive action (CAPA) system
3. Change management system
4. Management review

The document identifies components of those elements in some detail. The guidance also identifies knowledge management and quality risk management as critical enablers for the model.

Although a short document, ICH Q10 provides a wealth of good advice for any drug company interested in establishing a pharmaceutical QMS, particularly when combined with companion guidance documents, such as ICH Q8 on drug development[3] and ICH Q9 on quality risk management.[4]

## FDA MODELS

Some years earlier the FDA recognized that the quality management systems approach can help ensure pharmaceutical product quality. In February 2002, the FDA released the "Compliance Program Guidance Manual."[5] Quality System Inspection Technique (QSIT) inspection efficiencies created for inspections of medical device manufacturers apparently led to the desire for similar efficiencies with regard to inspections of drug manufacturers. A review of the FDA's current good management practice (CGMP) regulation, 21 CFR parts 210 and 211, led to an inspection approach looking at six systems:

1. Quality system: This includes the quality control unit and its review and approval duties, as well as product defect evaluations.
2. Facilities and equipment system.
3. Materials system.
4. Production system.
5. Packaging and labeling system.
6. Laboratory control system.

An inspection is defined in this manual as audit coverage of two or more systems, with mandatory coverage of Item 1, the quality system.

---

[3] International Conference on Harmonization of Technical Requirements for Pharmaceuticals for Human Use (ICH), "Guidance for Industry: Q8(R2) Pharmaceutical Development," November 2009, endorsed also by FDA Center for Drug Evaluation and Research (CDER) and Center for Biologics Evaluation and Research (CBER).

[4] International Conference on Harmonization of Technical Requirements for Pharmaceuticals for Human Use (ICH), "Guidance for Industry: Q9 Quality Risk Management," June 2006, endorsed also by FDA Center for Drug Evaluation and Research (CDER) and Center for Biologics Evaluation and Research (CBER).

[5] CPGM 7356.002, "Compliance Program—Drug Manufacturing Inspections," Issued 2/1/2002 (Minor revision 01/02/2015).

In September 2006, the FDA issued a guidance that described a quality system approach for drug GMP regulations that is in philosophy much like the (later) ICH Q10 model, although different in detail.

Rather than starting with the regulation and systematizing the regulation (as done in 2002), this effort started with a model much more like that of familiar international quality standards. It relates the sections of 21 CFR 211 with four key components:

- Management responsibilities
- Resources
- Manufacturing operations
- Evaluation activities

The similarity of this structure to that of ISO 13485 is clear. A detailed indication of the relationship of drug CGMPs to these subsystems is provided in Table A.1. The table also indicates how device regulations can fit this same outline.

The table shows both the strengths and weaknesses of the U.S. drug regulations. Strengths are the requirements for attention to detail in production. The weakness is a lack of actual requirements in key QMS areas, such as management review, internal audits, CAPA, and risk management.[6]

## CHOOSING A MODEL

Absent any need for relating to medical device regulations, a pharmaceutical company is likely to establish its PQS in accordance with the ICH Q10 model.

There are at least two instances when a company may need to create a QMS structure that relates to both device and drug regulations, namely:

- A company with both pharmaceutical and medical device divisions may determine that integration of the quality management systems into a single QMS will benefit the business.

---

[6] The FDA guidance document of course addresses only U.S. regulations. However, the statement is generally true with regard to drug regulations in other jurisdictions.

**TABLE A.1**

Details of FDA Pharma Quality System Model Based on 2006 Guidance Document

| Quality Systems Approach, Pharmaceutical CGMP Regulations | FDA Drug Regulations, particularly 21 CFR 211[7] | FDA Device Regulations, particularly 21 CFR 820 |
|---|---|---|
| **Management Responsibility** | | |
| 1. Provide Leadership | | 820.20 Management responsibility |
| | | 820.20(a) Quality policy |
| | | 820.20(c) Management review |
| 2. Structure the Organization | 211.22 Responsibilities of quality control unit (see definition § 210.3(b)(15)) | 820.20(b) Organization |
| | | 820.20(b)(1) Responsibility and authority |
| | 211.180 General requirements (for Records and Reports) | 820.20(b)(3) Management representative |
| 3. Build Quality System to Meet Requirements | Quality Unit procedures | Quality System |
| | 211.22 Responsibilities of quality control unit | 820.20(d) Quality planning |
| | Quality Unit procedures, specifications | 820.20(b)(1) Responsibility and authority |
| | 211.22 Responsibilities of quality control unit | 820.20(b)(2) Resources |
| | 211.100 Written procedures; deviations | 820.20(e) Quality system procedures |
| | 211.160 Laboratory controls, General requirements | 820.40 Document controls |
| | | 820.40(b) Document changes |
| | | *(Continued)* |

---

[7] Although the guidance document identifies the intended subsystem for most of the sections of 21 CFR 211 and other U.S. regulations applicable to pharmaceutical manufacturers, for a few cases not specified in the guidance, subsystems are proposed here. These items appear in italics.

**TABLE A.1 (*Continued*)**
Details of FDA Pharma Quality System Model Based on 2006 Guidance Document

| Quality Systems Approach, Pharmaceutical CGMP Regulations | FDA Drug Regulations, particularly 21 CFR 211 | FDA Device Regulations, particularly 21 CFR 820 |
| --- | --- | --- |
| | Quality Unit control steps | 820.20(b)(1) Responsibility and authority |
| | 211.22 Responsibilities of quality control unit | 820.250 Statistical techniques |
| | 211.42 Design and construction features | |
| | 211.84 Testing and approval or rejection of components, drug product containers, and closures | |
| | 211.87 Retesting of approved components, drug product containers, and closures | |
| | 211.101 Charge-in of components | |
| | 211.110 Sampling and testing of in-process materials and drug products | |
| | 211.115 Reprocessing | |
| | 211.142 Warehousing procedures | |
| | 211.165 Testing and release for distribution | |
| | 211.192 Production record review | |
| | Quality Unit quality assurance; review / investigate | 820.20(b) Organization |
| | 211.22 Responsibilities of quality control unit | |
| | 211.100 Written procedures; deviations | |
| | 211.180 General requirements (for Records and Reports) | |
| | 211.192 Production record review | |
| | 211.198 Complaint files | |

(*Continued*)

**TABLE A.1 (*Continued*)**

Details of FDA Pharma Quality System Model Based on 2006 Guidance Document

| Quality Systems Approach, Pharmaceutical CGMP Regulations | FDA Drug Regulations, particularly 21 CFR 211 | FDA Device Regulations, particularly 21 CFR 820 |
|---|---|---|
| | Record control | 11 Electronic Records and Electronic Signatures |
| | 11 Electronic Records and Electronic Signatures | 820.30(j) Design history file |
| | 211.180 General requirements (for Records and Reports) | 820.40 Document controls |
| | 211.184 Component, drug product container, closure, and labeling records | 820.180 General requirements |
| | 211.186 Master production and control records | 820.181 Device master record |
| | 211.188 Batch production and control records | 820.184 Device history record |
| | 211.192 Production record review | 820.186 Quality system record |
| | 211.194 Laboratory records | |
| | 211.196 Distribution records | |
| | 211.198 Complaint files | |
| 4. Establish Policies, Objectives and Plans | Procedures | 820.20(d) Quality planning |
| | 211.22 Responsibilities of quality control unit | |
| | 211.100 Written procedures; deviations | |
| 5. Review the System | Record review | 820.20(c) Management review |
| | 211.180 General requirements (for Records and Reports) | 820.80(d) Final acceptance activities |
| | 211.192 Production record review | 820.80(e) Acceptance records |
| | 211.198 Complaint files | 820.198 Complaint files |

*(Continued)*

**TABLE A.1 (*Continued*)**

Details of FDA Pharma Quality System Model Based on 2006 Guidance Document

| Quality Systems Approach, Pharmaceutical CGMP Regulations | FDA Drug Regulations, particularly 21 CFR 211 | FDA Device Regulations, particularly 21 CFR 820 |
|---|---|---|
| **Resources** | | |
| 1. General Arrangements | | 820.20(b) Organization |
| 2. Develop Personnel | Qualifications | 820.25 Personnel |
| | 211.25 Personnel qualifications | 820.25(a) [Personnel] General |
| | Staff number | 820.20(b) Organization |
| | 211.25 Personnel qualifications | |
| | Staff training | 820.25(b) Training |
| | 211.25 Personnel qualifications | 820.70(d) Personnel |
| 3. Facilities and Equipment | Buildings and facilities | 820.70(c) Environmental control |
| | 211.22 Responsibilities of quality control unit | 820.70(e) Contamination control |
| | 211.28 Personnel responsibilities | 820.70(f) Buildings |
| | 211.42 Design and construction features | 820.70(g) Equipment |
| | 211.44 Lighting | 820.72 Inspection, measuring, and test equipment |
| | 211.46 Ventilation, air filtration, air heating and cooling | |
| | 211.48 Plumbing | |
| | 211.50 Sewage and refuse | |
| | 211.52 Washing and toilet facilities | |
| | 211.56 Sanitation | |
| | 211.58 Maintenance | |
| | 211.173 Laboratory animals | |

*(Continued)*

**TABLE A.1 (*Continued*)**

Details of FDA Pharma Quality System Model Based on 2006 Guidance Document

| Quality Systems Approach, Pharmaceutical CGMP Regulations | FDA Drug Regulations, particularly 21 CFR 211 | FDA Device Regulations, particularly 21 CFR 820 |
|---|---|---|
| | Equipment | 820.70(g) Equipment |
| | 211.63 Equipment design, size and location | 820.72 Inspection, measuring, and test equipment |
| | 211.65 Equipment construction | |
| | 211.67 Equipment cleaning and maintenance | |
| | 211.68 Automatic, mechanical, and electronic equipment | |
| | 211.72 Filters | |
| | 211.105 Equipment identification | |
| | 211.160 General requirements (for Laboratory Controls) | |
| | 211.182 Equipment cleaning and use log | |
| | Lab facilities | 820.72 Inspection, measuring, and test equipment |
| | 211.22 Responsibilities of quality control unit | |
| 4. Control Outsourced Operations | Consultants | 820.50 Purchasing controls |
| | 211.34 Consultants | |
| | Outsourcing | 820.50 Purchasing controls |
| | 211.22 Responsibilities of quality control unit | |

*(Continued)*

**TABLE A.1 (*Continued*)**

Details of FDA Pharma Quality System Model Based on 2006 Guidance Document

| Quality Systems Approach, Pharmaceutical CGMP Regulations | FDA Drug Regulations, particularly 21 CFR 211 | FDA Device Regulations, particularly 21 CFR 820 |
| --- | --- | --- |
| **Manufacturing Operations** | | |
| 1. Design and Develop Product and Processes | Production<br>211.100 Written procedures; deviations<br>*211.166 Stability testing* | 820.30 Design Controls<br>820.30(a) General<br>820.30(b) Design and development planning<br>820.30(c) Design input<br>820.30(d) Design output<br>820.30(e) Design review<br>820.30(f) Design verification<br>820.30(g) Design validation<br>820.30(h) Design transfer<br>820.30(i) Design changes<br>820.70(b) Production and process changes<br>820.75 Process validation |
| 2. Monitor Packaging and Labeling Processes | *211.130 Packaging and labeling operations*<br>211.132 Tamper-evident packaging requirements for over-the-counter (OTC) human drug products<br>211.137 Expiration dating | 809 Labeling for In vitro Diagnostic Products<br>Device labeling<br>820.130 Device packaging |

(*Continued*)

**TABLE A.1 (*Continued*)**

Details of FDA Pharma Quality System Model Based on 2006 Guidance Document

| Quality Systems Approach, Pharmaceutical CGMP Regulations | FDA Drug Regulations, particularly 21 CFR 211 | FDA Device Regulations, particularly 21 CFR 820 |
|---|---|---|
| 3. Examine Inputs | Materials<br>210.3 Definitions<br>211.80 General requirements (for Control of components and drug product containers and closures)<br>211.82 Receipt and storage of untested components, drug product containers, and closures<br>211.84 Testing and approval or rejection of components, drug product containers, and closures<br>211.86 Use of approved components, drug product containers, and closures<br>211.87 Retesting of approved components, drug product containers, and closures<br>211.89 Rejected components, drug product containers, and closures<br>211.94 Drug product containers and closures<br>211.101 Charge-in of components<br>211.122 Materials examination and usage criteria<br>211.125 Labeling issuance | 820.50 Purchasing controls<br>820.50(a) Evaluation of suppliers, contractors, and consultants<br>820.50(b) Purchasing data<br>820.70(h) Manufacturing material<br>820.80(b) Receiving acceptance activities |

*(Continued)*

**TABLE A.1 (*Continued*)**
Details of FDA Pharma Quality System Model Based on 2006 Guidance Document

| Quality Systems Approach, Pharmaceutical CGMP Regulations | FDA Drug Regulations, particularly 21 CFR 211 | FDA Device Regulations, particularly 21 CFR 820 |
|---|---|---|
| 4. Perform and Monitor Operations | Production | 11 Electronic Records and Electronic Signatures |
| | 211.100 Written procedures; deviations | 820.60 Identification |
| | 211.103 Calculation of yield | 820.65 Traceability |
| | 211.110 Sampling and testing of in-process materials and drug products | 820.70 Production and process controls |
| | 211.111 Time limitations on production | 820.70(a) General |
| | 211.113 Control of microbiological contamination | 820.70(i) Automated processes |
| | *211.142 Warehousing procedures* | 820.140 Handling |
| | *211.150 Distribution procedures* | 820.150 Storage |
| | | 820.160 Distribution |
| | | 820.170 Installation |
| | | 820.200 Servicing |
| | QC criteria | 820.75 Process validation |
| | 211.22 Responsibilities of quality control unit | 820.80 Receiving, in-process, and finished device acceptance |
| | 211.115 Reprocessing | |
| | 211.160 General requirements (for Laboratory Controls) | |
| | 211.165 Testing and release for distribution | |

(*Continued*)

**TABLE A.1 (*Continued*)**

Details of FDA Pharma Quality System Model Based on 2006 Guidance Document

| Quality Systems Approach, Pharmaceutical CGMP Regulations | FDA Drug Regulations, particularly 21 CFR 211 | FDA Device Regulations, particularly 21 CFR 820 |
|---|---|---|
| | QC checkpoints | 820.80 Receiving, in-process, and finished device acceptance |
| | 211.22 Responsibilities of quality control unit | 820.80(a) General |
| | 211.84 Testing and approval or rejection of components, drug product containers, and closures | 820.80(c) In-process acceptance activities |
| | 211.87 Retesting of approved components, drug product containers, and closures | 820.80(d) Final acceptance activities |
| | 211.110 Sampling and testing of in-process materials and drug products | 820.80(e) Acceptance records |
| | *211.134 Drug product inspection* | 820.86 Acceptance status |
| | *211.166 Stability testing* | 820.170 Installation |
| | *211.167 Special testing requirements* | |
| | *211.170 Reserve samples* | |
| | *211.176 Penicillin contamination* | |
| 5. Address Nonconformities | Discrepancy investigation: | 803 Medical Device Reporting |
| | 211.22 Responsibilities of quality control unit | 820.90 Nonconforming product |
| | 211.115 Reprocessing | 820.90(a) Control of nonconforming product |
| | 211.192 Production record review | 820.90(b) Nonconforming review and disposition |
| | 211.198 Complaint files | 820.198 Complaint files |
| | Recalls | 806 Medical Devices; Reports of Corrections and Removals |
| | 7 Enforcement Policy | 7 Enforcement Policy |

*(Continued)*

**TABLE A.1 (*Continued*)**

Details of FDA Pharma Quality System Model Based on 2006 Guidance Document

| Quality Systems Approach, Pharmaceutical CGMP Regulations | FDA Drug Regulations, particularly 21 CFR 211 | FDA Device Regulations, particularly 21 CFR 820 |
|---|---|---|
| | *Returned and Salvaged Drug Products* | |
| | *211.204 Returned drug products* | |
| | *211.208 Drug product salvaging* | |
| **Evaluation Activities** | | |
| 1. Analyze Data for Trends | Annual Review 211.180 General requirements (for Records and Reports) | 820.250 Statistical techniques |
| 2. 2. Conduct Internal Audits | Annual Review 211.180 General requirements (for Records and Reports) | 820.22 Quality Audit |
| 3. Risk Assessment | | |
| 4. Corrective Action | Discrepancy investigation 211.22 Responsibilities of quality control unit 211.192 Production record review | 820.100 Corrective and preventive action |
| 5. Preventive Action | | 820.100 Corrective and preventive action |
| 6. Promote Improvement | | |

- A more likely scenario is one where a company is seeking marketing approval for a combination product, where the regulatory components for both the therapeutic agent and the device component must be in place.[8]

In such instances, a pharmaceutical company may find it useful to substitute the four key components of the QMS from the 2006 guidance in place of the four elements identified in ICH Q10. Such an approach may facilitate drug/device QMS harmonization because of the relationship noted above between the ISO 13485 structure and the structure presented in the 2006 FDA guidance.[9]

In the end, the model from either guidance document, or a mixture of elements from both can satisfy all requirements.

---

[8] See 21 CFR 4, "Regulation of Combination Products." Similar requirements apply in other jurisdictions.

[9] It seems ironic that the FDA-composed guidance document appears a better fit with the international device standard than the internationally composed guidance document.

# Appendix B: Addressing the Annex SL Model

As noted in Chapter 1 and again in Chapter 3, the Technical Management Board of ISO published Annex SL in 2012, which included a structure that all future quality management system (QMS) standards would be expected to use. The intent is to make it easier for companies wishing to implement more than one management standard, such as, for example, a company that wants to implement both a quality management standard and an environmental management standard. The intent of Appendix B is to show how a medical device company might address the Annex SL model in two different situations: (1) where the company seeks to address more than one type of management system, such as both quality and environmental; and (2) where the company seeks to maintain certification under the two quality management standards, both ISO 9001 and ISO 13485.

## MULTIPLE MANAGEMENT STANDARDS

The structure of Annex SL was implemented in the environmental management standard, ISO 14001:2015,[1] as well as the general quality management standard, ISO 9001:2015.[2] It will be used as well for the new ISO 45001 standard for Occupational Health and Safety.[3] ISO 9001:2015 places the elements of Annex SL in the context of the familiar Plan, Do, Check, Act (PDCA) cycle. See Figure B.1.

Figure B.1 is essentially the same as the figure used in ISO 9001:2015. The numbers in parentheses refer to clauses in the standard (see Table B.1). One change in the figure is that the phrase "satisfactory feedback" has been used on the right side of the figure in the place of the phrase "customer

---

[1] ISO 14001:2015, "Environmental management systems: Requirements with guidance for use."
[2] BS EN ISO 9001:2015, "Quality management systems: Requirements."
[3] ISO 45001:2018, "Occupational health and safety management systems—Requirements with guidance for use."

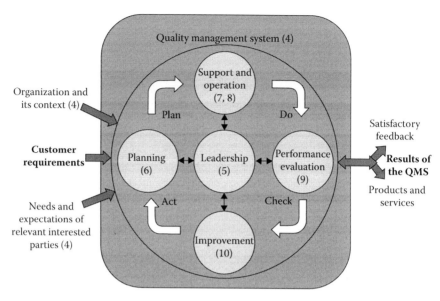

**FIGURE B.1**

Quality management system. (© ISO. This material is adapted from ISO 9001:2015 with permission of the American National Standards Institute (ANSI) on behalf of the International Organization for Standardization. All rights reserved.)

**TABLE B.1**

Relationship between Annex SL and ISO 13485:2016

| Annex SL | ISO 13485:2016 |
| --- | --- |
| 1. Scope | 1. Scope |
| 2. Normative references | 2. Normative references |
| 3. Terms and definitions | 3. Terms and definitions |
| 4. Context of the organization | 4. Quality management system |
| 5. Leadership | 5. Management responsibility |
| 6. Planning | 5.4.2 Quality management system planning |
| 7. Support | 6. Resource management |
| 8. Operation | 7. Product realization |
| 9. Performance evaluation | 8. Measurement, analysis, and improvement |
| 10. Improvement | 8.5 Improvement |

satisfaction." This replacement is intended to conform to the expectation of medical device regulatory authorities that customer satisfaction is not an appropriate concern for regulation.

Table B.1 describes in a general way how a company wishing to move to the Annex SL structure could do so and incorporate ISO 13485:2016.

**TABLE B.2**

High Level Documentation and the Annex SL Structure

| Annex SL Clause | Level 1 or Level 2 Procedure |
|---|---|
| 4. Context of the Organization | Quality Manual |
| 5. Leadership | Management Responsibility |
| 6. Planning | Management Responsibility |
| 7. Support | Documentation Management |
| | Records Management |
| | Qualification and Training |
| | Facilities and Equipment |
| | Software and Process Validation |
| 8. Operation | Risk Management |
| | Design Control |
| | Supplier Quality Management |
| | Product Regulatory Compliance |
| | Production |
| | Inspection, Test, Disposition |
| | Handling, Storage, Preservation, Delivery |
| | Service and Support |
| | Marketing and Sales |
| | Change Control |
| 9. Performance Evaluation | Management Responsibility |
| | Internal and External Audits |
| | Customer Feedback Management |
| 10. Improvement | Corrective and Preventive Action |
| | Control of Nonconforming Product |

Table B.2 shows how a company might allocate the high-level documentation discussed in chapters 5, 6, and 7 above to the clauses of an Annex SL structure.

Some comments are appropriate.

- Although Annex SL teaches away from the use of a quality manual, and the new ISO 9001 does not require a quality manual, in fact a quality manual is a quite appropriate home for material addressing the context for the organization and the general requirements for the QMS.
- The Level 2 procedure for management responsibility addresses subject matter for three clauses of the Annex SL model. This procedure can be divided to address each subject separately, but such a division should be avoided. Senior managers have quite wide-ranging

responsibilities for any business and normally carry heavy work-loads. It will be helpful to them to have a single Level 2 procedure that addresses their responsibilities with regard to the QMS.

- The Level 2 procedure for risk management is here assigned to the operation clause. This assignment is based on its content provided in Appendix C, which is focused on product risk. If this or a separate procedure were focused on business risk, it would be assigned to the clause on planning.

## TWO QUALITY MANAGEMENT STANDARDS

If the sole need for a company is to maintain certification to ISO 9001 and ISO 13485, there is no reason at the moment to change to the Annex SL structure. ISO 9001:2015 states clearly that there is no intention "to imply the need for uniformity in the structure of different quality management systems." This means that companies can find ways to be compliant with the new ISO 9001 within the framework of an ISO 13485 structure. Companies choosing to maintain certification to both ISO 9001 and ISO 13485 should address the new requirements of ISO 9001:2015 within their current structure. Annex B of ISO 13485:2016 provides useful information for the task. This kind of approach will minimize disruptions within the organization, and will allow many years for making the transition to an Annex SL structure—if indeed the company chooses to move in that direction.

A detailed examination of Annex SL and of ISO 9001:2015 reveals a significant disconnect from the regulatory philosophy behind ISO 13485. In Annex SL and in ISO 9001:2015 there is an increasing emphasis on improvement and a new focus on identifying and averting risks to the business. These are clearly benefits to any business, but are not appropriate areas for regulatory audits. Presumably, in the next revision of ISO 13485, the focus will be on finding ways to address the structural aspects of Annex SL without necessarily adopting its business philosophy.

# Appendix C: Example Level 2 Procedures

## GENERAL COMMENTS

The intent of Appendix C is not to spell out the details of all Level 2 requirements for any specific company, but rather to illustrate by example the idea of what should be the heart of this level of documentation. No claims are made for completeness with regard to the needs of any specific company.

As indicated in Chapter 3, the first step in the construction of Level 2 procedures should be the identification of the key processes for the company. These of course may be different from the list of processes used in this book; the guiding certainty is that the list must be able to encompass the scope of regulations and standards applicable to the company.

The next step will be the identification of all applicable requirements. This list will include:

- FDA requirements: 21 CFR 820, 21 CFR 803, 21 CFR 806, and other applicable regulations.
- International standards for quality management systems and product risk management: ISO 13485 and ISO 14971. Even companies not expecting to sell products outside the United States would benefit from fulfillment of the requirements of these standards. Fulfillment of ISO 13485 requirements ensures that the quality management system (QMS) will not require significant overhauling if/when the decision is made to sell outside the United States; until the decision is reached to sell outside the United States it may not be necessary to obtain registration to the standard. ISO 14971 will be useful in applying product risk management principles as expected by the U.S. Food and Drug Administration (FDA). Furthermore, fulfillment of requirements of ISO 13485:2016 will help ensure incorporation of risk management principles throughout the QMS.

- Additional requirements for regions and countries intended as markets, as indicated in Chapter 1.
- Additional standards chosen, such as ISO 9001.[1]
- Additional corporate requirements.

Once identified, the requirements must be incorporated in the appropriate Level 2 procedures. In most instances it is obvious which Level 2 procedure is the appropriate home for the requirement. In some cases it is a judgment call; the judgment should be made by keeping in mind particularly the users of the procedures. For example, following that user-driven logic in the following pages, principles for production documentation are included in the Level 2 procedure for production. Those principles could instead be appropriate for the procedure on documentation management.

It is possible to maintain the same requirement in two different procedures. However, this practice creates risks for change management of the procedures and should be avoided where possible.

Chapter 5 describes a technique that should be used to ensure full coverage of requirements in Level 2 documentation. Spreadsheets as described in that chapter will provide the quality and regulatory organizations with a complete view of the QMS documentation.

Note that the following examples are only covering the procedure or principles sections to be incorporated in this level of documentation, preceded by some commentary about responsibilities and scope. There are many additional sections that will be needed (see Chapter 5).

For most listed requirements, the entry begins with one or more reference in parenthesis, indicating the source for the requirement. In company procedures these references would normally be omitted.

- References reading "(21 CFR nnn.nn)" means the text is taken from the Code of Federal Regulations. These are usually from the Quality System Regulation, 21 CFR 820, and are by a wide margin the most

---

[1] Most medical device companies no longer maintain certification to ISO 9001. Since the ISO 9001:2015 has a structure different from ISO 13485:2016, it is likely that some companies currently maintaining certification to both will decide not to seek registration to ISO 9001:2015. For business reasons, some companies will continue certification to both quality standards. See Appendix B.

common references. Almost all requirements needed for a comprehensive QMS are found in the Quality System Regulation.

- Where a reference to the Preamble is added, this means that the Preamble to the Quality System Regulation contains information helpful in clarifying the intent of the requirement and therefore helpful in indicating what company procedures need to say.
- References reading "(ISO 13485, n.n)" indicate that ISO 13485:2016 has a requirement that goes beyond the requirements of the FDA's Quality System Regulation and that needs to be incorporated into company commitments if the intent is to market outside the United States.
- Footnotes reading "See also ISO 13485, n.n." are provided to indicate that the ISO 13485:2016 requirements identified are essentially the same as the requirements in the Quality System Regulation.
- ISO 13485 references in italics indicate new or modified requirements of ISO 13485:2016 compared with ISO 13485:2003.
- Because it is not possible in these examples to identify in all cases the responsible individual, group, or department, most of the requirements are stated in passive voice. In company procedures, it is preferable to find an active voice construction; active voice creates a higher level of urgency.

Most entries cover only the actual requirements from regulations and standards. However, there are some instances where practices have proved their usefulness even when not specifically required by quality standard or regulation. There are also a few instances where provisions are provided for dealing with current and anticipated practices for notified bodies with regard to implementation of new regulatory practices in Europe. These provisions are annotated accordingly.

The examples of Appendix C do not address some subject areas that a company may want to include in Level 2 procedures, although not required explicitly by any standard or regulation. For instance, the example procedure for management responsibility does not include a section to spell out expected responsibilities of a Quality Council. Nevertheless, the management responsibility procedure would be the correct home for describing those responsibilities (see Chapter 4).

---

## MANAGEMENT RESPONSIBILITY

### Responsibilities[2]

*The responsibility for most of the requirements for this process will lie with senior management. Multiple administrative tasks involved, such as data collection, analysis, and presentation for management review are normally assigned to the quality organization. In this and other Level 2 procedures, the regulatory organization should be responsible for identification and interpretation of regulatory requirements. The management responsibilities should be clearly stated. As noted above, this is the right procedure to define responsibilities of a quality council.*

### Requirements

#### General

1. (21 CFR 820.5)[3] A QMS shall be established[4] that meets requirements of applicable regulations and standards and is appropriate for company products. (ISO 13485, 4.1.1) *The company role(s) under applicable regulations shall be defined.*
2. (ISO 13485, 8.5.1) Changes necessary for ongoing effectiveness of the QMS shall be implemented through use of QMS elements, such as policy, objectives, audits, data analysis, corrective and preventive actions, and management review.
3. (21 CFR 820.20(a))[5] A quality policy shall be established and actions shall be taken to ensure that this policy is understood, implemented, and maintained at all levels of the company. This quality policy shall:
   • (ISO 13485, 5.3 a)) Suit the company purpose

---

[2] It is reasonable to assign responsibility for all items in this category to the senior management team. If a company believes it is appropriate to assign some of these responsibilities differently, the applicable regulation or quality standard should be consulted, because some of the items are required to be addressed by senior management.

[3] See also ISO 13485, 4.1.

[4] For the sake of brevity, statements in Appendix C use the word "establish" to stand for the phrase "establish and maintain." With appropriate documentation, external auditors should find this approach acceptable in company procedures.

[5] See also ISO 13485, 4.2.1 a), 5.1 b), and 5.3 d).

- (ISO 13485, 5.3 b)) Commit to compliance and maintenance of QMS effectiveness[6]
- (ISO 13485, 5.3 c)) Provide a basis for addressing quality objectives.[7]

(ISO 13485, 5.3 e)) The quality policy must be assessed for ongoing suitability.

4. (21 CFR 820.20(a))[8] and (ISO 13485, 5.4.1) Measurable quality objectives shall be established appropriate to the quality policy. These objectives must include objectives related to meeting product requirements and must be established for the appropriate departments, and at the appropriate levels within those departments.

5. (ISO 13485, 5.5.3) Communication processes shall be established in support of the QMS that ensure communication of:
   - (ISO 13485, 5.2) The importance of identifying customer requirements and meeting them
   - (ISO 13485, 5.1 a, 5.2) The importance of identifying and meeting applicable regulatory requirements
   - (ISO 13485, 5.5.3) The ongoing effectiveness of the QMS

## Organization

1. (21 CFR 820.20(b)) An adequate organizational structure shall be established to ensure that products are designed and produced meeting applicable requirements.

2. (21 CFR 820.20(b)(1)) Appropriate responsibility, authority, and interrelation of personnel whose work affects quality shall be established, and the independence and authority necessary to perform these tasks shall be provided. (ISO 13485, 5.5.1) This information shall be communicated throughout the company.

---

[6] One approach that can be used to meet this objective is for the quality policy to commit to fulfillment of customer requirements and then to include regulatory authorities among the groups designated as customers. This requires ongoing training to ensure that company employees are aware of this designation of regulatory authorities. Although some quality system registrars may not be comfortable with this approach, the 2016 standard appears to support it. In ISO 13485:2016, Clause 5.2, entitled "Customer focus," addresses both customer and regulatory requirements.

[7] It would not be unusual for an auditor from a registrar to expect to see objective evidence (possibly in the form of metrics) that can show the extent to which the company is fulfilling the commitments of the quality policy.

[8] See also ISO 13485, 4.2.1 a), 5.1 b).

3. Individuals shall be appointed to specific positions required by national or regional regulations for oversight of specified aspects of the QMS that ensure products and processes meet requirements.[9]

4. (ISO 13485, 4.1.2, 4.1.3) Processes needed for the QMS and appropriate to the organization's roles shall be established throughout the organization *using a risk-based approach for their control.* Their interactions shall be defined. Actions needed to ensure their effectiveness shall be determined. Resources shall be provided for carrying out the processes effectively and monitoring them to ensure ongoing effectiveness in meeting requirements of applicable regulations and standards.

5. (ISO 13485, 4.1.3, 8.1 b), c), 8.2.5, 8.4) Processes shall be monitored and measured with appropriate methods, including statistical techniques, to demonstrate ability to achieve planned results and ensure conformity, suitability, adequacy, and effectiveness of the QMS;[10] records shall be maintained. Appropriate corrective or preventive actions shall be taken when needed to achieve planned results and ensure product conformity.

### Resources

1. (21 CFR 820.20(b)(2))[11] Adequate resources shall be provided, including assignment of trained, competent personnel for management, performance of work, and assessment activities, including internal quality audits, to:
   - Implement the QMS and maintain its effectiveness
   - Meet regulatory and customer requirements.

2. (21 CFR 820.70 (c), (f), (g), (i))[12] Infrastructure needed to meet product requirements shall be established, including:
   - Buildings, including utilities
   - Equipment, including software
   - Support services, including information systems

---

[9] This is particularly important with regard to the requirement for qualified persons in new European device regulations.

[10] Most companies will want to specify in their Level 2 procedure the further details enumerated in ISO 13485, 8.4.

[11] See also ISO 13485, 5.1 e), 6.1 for both 1. and 2.

[12] See also ISO 13485, 6.3.

## Management Representative

1. (21 CFR 820.20(b)(3)) Appointment[13] shall be documented of a member of management who, irrespective of other responsibilities is responsible for:
   - Ensuring that QMS requirements are effectively established and maintained to meet applicable requirements
   - (ISO 13485, 5.5.2) Ensuring QMS processes are appropriately identified and executed
   - Reporting on the performance of the QMS and any needs for improvement
   - (ISO 13485, 5.5.2) Promoting awareness of regulatory and *quality management system* requirements throughout the company
2. Appointment of deputy management representative(s) shall be documented as needed to fulfill management representative responsibilities.[14]

## Quality Planning[15]

1. (21 CFR 820.20(d)) A quality plan shall be established that defines the quality practices, resources, and activities relevant to products that are designed and manufactured, and that establishes how the requirements for quality will be met.[16]
2. (ISO 13485, 5.4.2 a, 8.1)) Adequate quality planning for the QMS shall be ensured, including the creation of quality plans as needed for meeting objectives and requirements for established processes.[17]

---

[13] It is usually simplest for the president to have responsibility for making this appointment. It may be useful to use the Level 2 procedure on management responsibility to document the position that is designated as management representative, often the head of the quality function.

[14] Not a requirement of a standard or regulation, but a useful practice. It is particularly useful for multisite organizations combined into a single quality system. It is useful for the management representative to have responsibility for designating the deputies.

[15] Responsibility for quality planning normally should be assigned on an ad hoc basis, with senior management responsible to ensure that it is being carried out when required/appropriate.

[16] This FDA use of the term "quality plan" is not as clear as might be desired. It seems that the quality plan of the FDA could be simply the device master record (DMR), but if the DMR alone would satisfy the requirement it is hard to understand why there are two separate sections in the regulation. Perhaps it may be defined as the applicable DMR plus the quality system record or plus the quality system documentation as a whole. The company should document its own interpretation of how it is meeting this requirement in case an inspector chooses to raise a question.

[17] "ISO 13485:2016, Medical devices: A practical guide," provides guidance on meeting this requirement. It may be useful to create an ongoing plan for quality improvement of both products and the QMS that brings together the various activities established via customer feedback, CAPA, NC Product, etc.

3. (ISO 13485, 4.1.4, 5.4.2 b)) The integrity of the QMS shall be maintained when changes are planned and implemented. *Changes shall be evaluated for impact on product and on the QMS, and shall be carried out according to requirements of applicable standards and regulations.* Substantial changes to the QMS or the range of products shall be communicated as required.[18]

### Management Review

1. (21 CFR 820.20(c))[19] The suitability and effectiveness of the QMS shall be reviewed [specify frequency] to ensure that the QMS fulfills applicable requirements and the established quality policy and objectives. See Attachment A for management review requirements.
2. (21 CFR 820.20(c)) Materials for management review shall be prepared and results and dates shall be documented.[20]
3. Subreviews may be authorized explicitly where appropriate.[21]

## Attachment A: Management Review Requirements[22]

Requirements for ISO 13485[23]

a. General
b. Input[24]
c. Output
d. Summary statement on QMS status[25]

---

[18] European directives and regulations require that substantial changes to the quality system be reported to the registrar/notified body that has evaluated the quality system. There may be similar requirements in other jurisdictions.

[19] See also ISO 13485, 5.1 (d), 5.6.1.

[20] Responsibility normally of the management representative.

[21] Not a requirement of a standard or regulation, but a useful practice for larger companies. This may be done on the basis of geography, organizational structure, or subject matter. It may also be helpful to use subreviews to provide for more frequent review of certain data.

[22] It is useful for the procedure on management review to have a listing of the sources of all the detailed requirements for management review, together with a listing of the required subjects. In particular it is important to list from ISO 13485 the specific requirements of 5.6. The agenda, however, should be ordered as appropriate to facilitate effective review.

[23] It will be useful to refer to ISO 13485 8.1 and 8.2.1 in preparing for management review. "ISO 13485:2016, Medical devices: A practical guide" has much good advice for this subject.

[24] In preparation of the agenda for the review it is prudent to include specific references to regions and countries whose regulations are intended to be met by the QMS requirements, such as Europe, Canada, Australia, Japan, China, etc., particularly when external QMS audits may include explicitly the requirements from those regions/countries.

[25] Not explicitly stated in the standard but generally expected by auditors. There needs to be evidence that this assessment is not simply perfunctory. One company asks each participant to rate the status of the QMS and then averages the ratings to reach a conclusion.

Requirements for 21 CFR 820.20(c)

  e. Suitability and effectiveness of the QMS
  f. Fulfillment of requirements of 21 CFR 820
  g. Fulfillment of requirements of the quality policy
  h. Fulfillment of quality objectives

Requirements for ISO 14971[26]

  i. Continuing suitability of risk management process

Other requirements

  j. In accordance with company requirements[27]

---

## PRODUCT RISK MANAGEMENT[28,29,30]

### Responsibilities

*Senior management has responsibility for establishing and maintaining the product risk management system as specified in Item 2 below. Most of the responsibility for product risk management in product development will be assigned to research and development. Postproduction responsibility will usually rest with the quality and/or regulatory function.*

---

[26] Assumes that fulfillment of ISO 14971 requirements is an expectation for the QMS. Given that risk management principles are present throughout ISO 13485:2016, the subject of the risk management process can be considered an appropriate requirement for management review whether or not the company has a specific commitment to ISO 14971.

[27] For example, a company may choose to make the subject of possible product discontinuation an agenda item for management review. (This would be for reasons not related to product safety, since product safety–related questions would be addressed in a more timely manner through the customer feedback management process.)

[28] Although as a result of the impact of ISO 13485:2016 the entire QMS is required to incorporate risk management principles for all processes, there is value to a Level 2 procedure devoted specifically to product risk management.

[29] The items included here are the most critical aspects of product risk management. A company striving for full compliance with ISO 14971 may wish to address requirements of the standard in more detail in its Level 2 procedure.

[30] If risk management is formalized for the business as a whole, incorporating a variety of business-related risks, the business risks should be clearly separated from the product risks so that external auditors' examination of business risks may be avoided.

## Requirements

1. (ISO 14971, 3.1) The risk management process shall include:
   - Analysis for risks
   - Evaluation of risks
   - Control of risks
   - Overall evaluation of residual risks
   - Monitoring of risks in production and in the marketplace
2. (ISO 14971, 3.2) Senior management shall ensure:
   - Adequate resources for management of risk
   - Qualified individuals for management of risk
   - Establishment of policy for risk criteria acceptability
   - Periodic review of the process for risk management
3. In management of risk, the following principles shall be applied in the priority order listed:[31]
   a. Identify known or foreseeable hazards and estimate the associated risks arising from the intended use and foreseeable misuse.
   b. Eliminate risks as far as possible (without adversely affecting the benefit-risk ratio), through inherently safe design and manufacture.
   c. Reduce as far as possible the remaining risks by taking adequate protection measures, including alarms.
   d. Provide training to users and/or inform users of any residual risk. Note that the provision of information to customers does not reduce the actual risk.
4. In the overall assessment of residual risks, the benefits shall outweigh the known and foreseeable risks as well as undesirable side effects.[32] This benefit/risk assessment shall be documented for each product.
5. (ISO 14971, 3.5, 7, 8) A risk management file shall be established for each product that provides evidence of compliance with applicable

---

[31] It should be noted that current requirements in the Medical Device Directive and the IVD Directive are more stringent and do not contain the phrase "without adversely affecting the benefit-risk ratio," which was added in the new European regulations. Until these new regulations are fully in force, each company should contact its notified body to clarify the expected interpretation.

[32] 93/42/EEC, Medical Devices Directive, Annex I, I, 1; 98/79/EC, *In Vitro* Diagnostic Medical Devices Directive, Annex I, A, 1; Regulation 2017/745 (MDR), Annex I, Chapter I; Regulation 2017/746 (IVDR), Annex I, Chapter I.

requirements, including measures for controlling risks, the overall evaluation of residual risks and the risk management report.[33]

6. (ISO 14971, 9) Postmarket information shall be reviewed to determine whether the risk information in the risk management file is correct or whether it must be revised on the basis of further experience.

---

# DOCUMENTATION MANAGEMENT

## Responsibilities

*The quality department should oversee documentation, although it may be appropriate for other departments to manage specified types of documentation. For example, it may be appropriate for the research and development department to have responsibility for creation and maintenance of engineering drawings.*

*It can be acceptable for individual departments to have control of work instructions that affect only that department. However, the quality department should always be aware of the existence of these departmental systems in order to ensure that they are correctly managed. It is usually preferable to have a general system overseen and managed by the quality department that allows individual departments to create their own work instructions.*

## Requirements

### General

1. (21 CFR 820.20(e), 820.40) and (ISO 13485, 4.2.1 d), e)) QMS procedures and instructions shall be established, including:
   - Documentation to ensure effectiveness of QMS processes
   - Documentation arising from regulatory requirements where products are to be sold
2. (21CFR820.20(e)) and (ISO 13485, 4.1.1, 4.2.1 b), c), 4.2.2, 4.2.4) Procedures shall be established to control all required QMS documents, that is, those documents necessary to meet regulatory and

---

[33] An excellent summary of ISO 14971 requirements for the risk management file is found in PLUS 14971, "The ISO 14971:2007 essentials: A practical handbook for implementing the ISO 14971 Standard for medical devices," Canadian Standards Association, Mississauga, Ontario, Canada, 2007.

quality standard requirements. Primary among procedures is a quality manual that includes:

- *The role(s) for the organization under applicable regulations, such as manufacturer, importer, or distributor*[34]
- QMS scope, including explanations for any exemptions from requirements of regulations and standards[35]
- An outline of QMS documentation, including reference to procedures[36]
- The interaction of QMS processes

3. (21 CFR 820.40(a))[37] Established procedures shall ensure designation of individual(s) to:

- Review QMS documents for adequacy
- Approve QMS documents prior to issuance, by signature and date

4. (21 CFR 820.40(a), (b))[38] Established procedures shall ensure:

- That documentation is reviewed and updated as necessary and, where appropriate, re-approved[39]
- That changes and current revision status are identified
- That documents remain legible and identifiable

5. (21 CFR 820.40(a))[40] Established procedures shall ensure:

- That QMS documents are available at all locations for which they are designated, used, or otherwise necessary
- That all obsolete documents are promptly removed from points of use or otherwise prevented from unintended use, and are identified if retained for any reason

---

[34] ISO 13485 does not specify that this information must be in the manual, but this is its logical home.

[35] Note that ISO 13485 requires a distinction between two different kinds of exemption: exclusion (related to elements in sections 6, 7, or 8 of ISO 13485:2016) and nonapplicability (related to the kinds of products produced). Section 7.3 would be excluded, for example, for a contract manufacturer that does not do design control. A company that does not have any sterile products would declare that sections of the standard addressing sterility are not applicable to that company.

[36] It is also acceptable for the procedures to be included in the manual. However, that approach would defeat one of the purposes of the manual, as described in Chapter 6, and should not be used.

[37] See also ISO 13485, 4.2.4 a).

[38] See also ISO 13485, 4.2.4 b), c), e), g).

[39] Re-approval would be appropriate where a periodic review of the document is required, but where the review indicates no need to change the document. The re-approval constitutes the objective evidence that the review took place.

[40] See also ISO 13485, 4.2.4 d), h).

6. (ISO 13485, 4.2.4 f)) Established procedures shall ensure that documents of external origin are identified and controlled.[41]
7. Delegation of responsibility for fulfilling procedure requirements is permitted except where explicitly forbidden.[42]

### *Document Changes*

1. (21 CFR 820.40(b)) Changes to documents shall be reviewed and approved by an individual(s) in the same function or organization that performed the original review and approval, unless specifically designated otherwise. ISO 13485, 4.2.4) If designated otherwise, the designated function must have access to necessary background information.
2. (21 CFR 820.40(b)) Approved changes shall be communicated to the appropriate personnel in a timely manner.
3. (21 CFR 820.40(b)) Records of changes to documents shall be maintained. Change records shall include:
   - A description of the change
   - Identification of the affected documents
   - The signature of the approving individual(s)
   - The approval date
   - The date when the change becomes effective

## RECORDS MANAGEMENT

### Responsibilities

*The quality department should oversee records, although it will be appropriate for other departments to manage various types of records. Research and development may maintain design records. Sales may maintain records of*

---

[41] Often the most extensive group of external documents to be controlled is the collection of design standards. The research and development department may be the most appropriate group to control these standards.

[42] This provision may be omitted in the Level 2 documentation procedure if it is present in the manual. Although not required by quality standard or regulation, it removes the need for explicit statements permitting delegation in a large number of procedures.

shipments. *Manufacturing may keep maintenance records. Thus, General Item 2 is important, not because it is explicitly required by regulation or standard, but because most departments have some sort of quality record(s) ("Quality is everyone's business.") and the records will be better cared for when the responsibility for them is acknowledged.*

*The information technology function should have some responsibilities related to electronic records. If this function is outsourced, these responsibilities should be managed by the quality function through supplier quality management.*

## Requirements

### *General*

1. (21 CFR 820.180)[43] Records providing evidence of conformity to requirements of QMS procedures[44] shall be maintained at secure locations that are reasonably accessible to company employees responsible for their creation and use.
2. Department managers shall ensure that QMS records generated by that department are identified in writing, and that controlled locations for these records have been defined.
3. (21 CFR 820.180) QMS records shall be maintained at secure locations that are reasonably accessible to representatives of regulatory authorities, quality standard registrars, and other agencies designated to perform QMS inspections. Such records, including electronic records and including records not stored at the inspected facility, shall be made readily available for review and copying by regulatory authorities, quality standard registrars, and other agencies designated to perform QMS inspections.

    (21 CFR 820.180(c)) Exceptions: Records of management review, quality audit reports, and supplier audit reports shall not normally be made available to FDA investigators,[45] although copies of applicable procedures shall be provided upon request. Upon request of a designated employee of the FDA, an employee in management with executive responsibility shall certify in writing that

---

[43] See also ISO 13485, 4.2.5.

[44] Because QMS procedures implement standards and regulations, this statement ensures by implication that records required by those standards and regulations will be created and maintained.

[45] It may be appropriate to include in the procedure advice on what to do (such as seek legal advice) in the unlikely event that the FDA investigator insists on seeing these records.

the management reviews and quality audits required by 21 CFR 820, and supplier audits where applicable, have been performed and documented, the dates on which they were performed, and that any required corrective action has been undertaken.[46]

4. (21 CFR 820.180)[47] QMS records shall meet basic requirements.[48]
   - Records shall be legible, readily identifiable, and retrievable.
   - Records shall be created in black or blue ink, not pencil.
   - Corrections, when needed, shall be made by drawing a single line in ink through the corrected material and adding correct information with signature or initials and date.
   - (ISO 13485, 4.2.5) *Changes to records shall be identifiable.*
   - Records shall be stored to minimize deterioration and to prevent loss.[49]

5. Accessibility to quality records shall be limited to individuals necessary to fulfill quality, regulatory, and business needs.[50]

6. (21 CFR 820.180(a)) Confidentiality of quality records shall be maintained as appropriate. Records provided to regulatory authorities to be taken off the premises that are deemed confidential may be marked to aid regulatory authorities in determining whether information may be disclosed under applicable regulations.[51] (45 CFR 160, 162, 164) Confidential health information shall be protected.[52]

7. In the unlikely event that a quality record becomes contaminated by a body fluid, the record shall be retained in a manner consistent with both safety and quality/regulatory requirements.[53]

8. In the event of organizational changes, planning for quality shall include transition of responsibility for records.[54]

---

[46] The FDA is entitled to see evidence that these requirements have been met. There can be alternative approaches to the certification in writing. For example, the management review minutes can be formatted such that the first page includes only the date, the attendees, and the agenda. Then the first page can be shown to an FDA investigator and the subsequent pages remain confidential.

[47] See also ISO 13485, 4.2.5.

[48] Some of these items are not explicitly required by quality standards or regulation.

[49] If thermal printouts are used, it may be advisable to specify that the printout be copied and retained with the original, since the thermal printout is likely to fade before the retention time has elapsed.

[50] This is a business requirement, not a quality or regulatory requirement. One alternative to this approach would be for the company to establish various levels of confidentiality.

[51] In particular, see 21 CFR 20.

[52] See also ISO 13485, 4.2.5.

[53] Not addressed by quality standards or regulation.

[54] Implicitly required by quality standards or regulation.

9. (21 CFR 820.186) The quality manual, together with Level 2 procedures and Level 3 procedures that are not product-specific, as well as the resulting records fulfill the requirement for a "quality system record" as defined in 21 CFR 820.186.[55]

### Retention and Disposition

1. Retention times for QMS records, including electronic records, are defined in Attachment A. Attachment A incorporates retention requirements of applicable regulatory authorities, including[56]

   - (21 CFR 820.180(b)) The FDA requirement that records be retained for a period of time equivalent to the design and expected life of the product, but in no case less than two years from the date of release for commercial distribution.

   - EU requirements that specified records be maintained for a specified period after manufacture of the last product: 10 years for in vitro diagnostic devices and nonimplantable medical devices[57] and 15 years for implantable and active implantable medical devices.

   - (ISO 13485, 4.2.4) The quality standard requirement that at least one copy of obsolete documents be retained for the lifetime of the product,[58] but not less than the retention period requirement for any resulting record or as required by regulatory authorities.

   - (ISO 13485, 4.2.5) The quality standard requirement that product-related records be kept for the longest time among: (1) the lifetime of the product; (2) 2 years from product release; or (3) period specified by a regulatory authority.

2. Disposition/destruction of records shall be carried out in accordance with the time requirements specified in Attachment A. Provision

---

[55] This provision may be omitted in the Level 2 records procedure if it is present in the manual. Other, similar wording may meet the requirement.

[56] These details may alternatively be incorporated as footnotes to the attachment.

[57] Under the MDD and the IVDD this was five years. This was changed with the MDR and the IVDR.

[58] Note that this implies a requirement that the lifetime of the product be specified. See useful advice in "ISO 13485:2016, Medical devices: A practical guide, 2017."

shall be made to ensure that confidential records are destroyed in a manner that ensures no breach of confidentiality.

3. Records and other documents may be stored with an external service provider that is able to fulfill requirements[59]:

   • Protection and security
   • Ability to supply records within a reasonable time upon request (normally < 24 hours)
   • Ability to provide confidential destruction and certificates of destruction

   Records and other documentation stored with an external service shall be identified adequately to allow retrieval and/or destruction as needed.

### Electronic Records[60]

1. Either electronic or paper copies of records may be used to support fulfillment of regulatory requirements, unless a regulation specifically requires either paper or electronic records.

   • (21 CFR 11.10(j)) Individuals signing electronic records shall treat their electronic signature with the same respect as their handwritten signature.
   • (21 CFR 11.100(c)) The company has certified to the FDA that electronic signatures are intended to be the legally binding equivalent of traditional handwritten signatures.[61]

2. (21 CFR 11.10) Systems used to create, modify, maintain, or transmit electronic records shall be designed, validated and maintained in a manner that ensures authenticity, integrity, accuracy, and reliability of the records, and shall comply with regulatory requirements for electronic records. See FDA "Guidance for Industry, Part 11, Electronic Records; Electronic Signatures: Scope and Application,"

---

[59] Some of these items are not explicitly required by quality standards or regulation.

[60] Although 21 CFR 11 and subsequent guidance address the important issues for medical device companies, such companies may also wish to heed European Annex 11, which is aimed at medicinal products, particularly for combination products.

[61] Ensure that a copy of the certification letter is readily available in case of FDA investigation.

August 2003. Security may be based on network security or on specific software applications.[62]

3. (21 CFR 11.30) If the system for electronic records is an open system, where system access is controlled external to the company, procedures and controls shall ensure record authenticity, integrity, and confidentiality, using, as appropriate, measures such as document encryption.[63]

4. Electronic records may be approved with handwritten signatures provided that the integrity of the approved electronic record is controlled. Such records may be printed out, reviewed, and approved by handwritten signature. Such records shall be retained in the same manner as paper records.

5. (21 CFR 820.180) Records stored in electronic systems shall be backed up.

6. Where electronic systems are used and have been validated, intermediate data from the electronic system need not be controlled as an electronic record. Data become electronic records at the first act of storage to a medium to be saved for later processing or evaluation.[64]

7. Regulatory affairs or the legal department should be consulted in the event of questions concerning applicability of principles for ensuring integrity of electronic records.

   • Exceptions to specific requirements may be permitted with documented rationale approved by regulatory affairs.
   • If there are questions regarding the ability of the regulatory agency to perform review and copying of electronic records, the regulatory agency should be contacted.

---

[62] It is useful at this point to be able to refer to an attachment tailored to company practices and company interpretation of regulations for electronic records and signatures that addresses the requirements for electronic records in more detail. It is not practical here to specify the details of regulatory expectations that will be appropriate for all companies. Nevertheless, if one recognizes the fundamental requirement to be the preservation of record integrity for the lifetime of the record, it is normally possible for each company to find practical approaches that meet this basic need.

[63] With the general increase in the use of cloud storage, as well as the general increase in hacking incidents, this provision deserves particular attention. The company may decide it is wiser to allow only the use of closed systems.

[64] This is not explicitly found in a regulation. Nevertheless, a statement of this nature may be useful for documenting intentions with regard to the thousands of data points that can be collected with process-monitoring equipment. It will not normally be practical to treat each of these data points as an electronic record.

# ATTACHMENT A

Record Retention Table[65]

| No. | Item | Retention Time[66] |
|-----|------|--------------------|
| 1 | Management Review Minutes | 7 years |
| 2 | Internal Audit Reports | 7 years |
| 3 | Training Records | Seven years after the end of employment |
| 4 | Design History File, Technical File | 10 years longer than the date of last product manufacture |
| 5 | Complaint Files | 10 years longer than the date of last product manufacture |
| 6 | CAPA | 10 years longer than the date of last product manufacture |
| 7 | Corrections and removals | 10 years longer than the date of last product manufacture |
| 8 | Device History Records | 10 years after the expiration date for products with expiration dates and 10 years longer than the date of last product manufacture for products without expiration dates |
| 9 | Device Master Records | 10 years longer than the date of last product manufacture |
| 10 | Validation Reports | 10 years longer than the date of last product manufacture |
| 11 | Regulatory Decisions, including decisions and reports of the Notified Body | 10 years longer than the date of last product manufacture |
| 12 | Supplier File | 10 years after last materials/service supplied |
| 13 | Distribution/Consignee records | Storage life of product plus two years |

---

[65] This table is intended to provide a general example of the types of records possible and the retention times that might be allocated. In an actual Level 2 procedure, a company would identify all types of records required to demonstrate fulfillment of requirements. This will include records for QMS processes, as required in ISO 13485:2016, 4.1.3. In determining the retention times, the company would also determine where applicable regulatory requirements supersede the inclination to dispose of records as quickly as possible.

An additional required column for the table (not shown here) is a column to designate the department responsible for the particular type of record.

[66] Seven years allows for one year past two recertification cycles for ISO 13485. The 10-year time requirement would become 15 years if the products involved were implantable.

Although some companies like to use the term "indefinite" for retention periods, most registrars do not find this term satisfactory. "Indefinite with X year review" may be more acceptable, although use of this phrase should involve a clear explanation of the process for deciding whether or not the record can be discarded at the X year review. The approved supplier list is clearly a record that requires an indefinite retention period. However, registrars that will not accept indefinite as a retention period may allow the ASL to be defined as not a record (with supplier records being the materials in each supplier's file). Companies need to work with third-party auditors to clarify details regarding retention times.

## INTERNAL AND EXTERNAL AUDITS

### Responsibilities

*The quality function usually has responsibility for the administration of internal audits and for planning related to external audits. Each department must be responsible for responding in a timely manner to any findings.*

### Requirements

#### Internal Audits

1. (21 CFR 820.22)[67] A system of quality audits at planned intervals shall be established by procedure(s) to assure that the QMS is in compliance with the established QMS requirements, including applicable regulatory requirements,[68] and to determine the effectiveness of the QMS. The system shall include:
   - Definition of responsibility for planning and carrying out audits, for reporting results, and for maintaining audit records
   - Definition of audit scope and audit frequency in a manner that ensures addressing the full scope of the QMS within a reasonable time frame
   - Definition of criteria for audits, as well as methods to be used by auditors
2. (ISO 13485, 8.2.4) Audit planning shall take into consideration the importance of the processes/groups audited and outcomes of previous audits.
3. (21 CFR 820.22) Auditor selection and conduct of audits shall ensure objectivity and impartiality. In particular, audits shall be conducted by individuals who do not have direct responsibility for the matters being audited.
4. (21 CFR 820.22) The dates and results of quality audits and re-audits shall be documented.

---

[67] See also ISO 13485, 8.2.4 for both 1 and 3.

[68] Particularly with the MDSAP program in place, companies should expect external auditors to determine whether internal audits address regulatory issues in countries where products are sold.

### External Audits[69]

1. Actions shall be taken with registrars and regulatory authorities to ensure that external audits are planned and conducted in an effective and efficient manner.
2. Procedures shall be established to address coverage of unannounced audits by notified bodies or other regulatory authorities.
3. Procedures shall be established to ensure communication of external audit results to senior management.[70]

### Audit Follow-Up

1. (21 CFR 820.22) A report of the results of each internal quality audit, and re-audits where taken, shall be made.
2. (21 CFR 820.22) and (ISO 13485, 8.2.4) Management having responsibility for the matters audited shall review and respond to audit reports, both internal and external, in a timely manner and shall ensure that nonconformities are addressed in a timely manner by correction or corrective action as required.[71]
3. (21 CFR 820.22) Corrective actions, including a re-audit of deficient matters, shall be taken when necessary.[72]
4. (21 CFR 820.100(a)(4) Follow-up shall include verification of the actions taken to deal with nonconformities and shall include documentation of this verification.

# QUALIFICATION AND TRAINING

### Responsibilities

*In the ideal case, human resources should be responsible for the general administration of training records, not only related to quality and job performance, but also related to safety, to financial compliance, to ethics, etc.*

---

[69] Not addressed explicitly by quality standards or regulation.

[70] Companies with multiple sites should include a provision that external audit results be communicated also to other sites.

[71] In determining whether a correction or a corrective action is required, criteria are normally defined in the CAPA procedures.

[72] Normally a re-audit would be part of an effectiveness check for a corrective action.

*Unfortunately, in many companies the quality department is left by default with administrative responsibility for quality training.*

*Management of each department should be responsible to identify training needs and for the assessment of whether those needs have been met.*

*Although not specifically required by regulation or standard, it may be useful to make the quality council responsible for identifying training needs for the QMS during the year.*

## Requirements

### Qualifications

1. (21 CFR 820.25(a))[73] Established procedures shall ensure that personnel carrying out activities required by the QMS have the necessary education, background, training, and experience to assure that those activities are correctly performed.[74]
2. (21 CFR 820.25(a), (b)) Competency requirements for individuals performing work affecting product quality shall be established, including:
   • Education and skills
   • Background and experience
   • Training, including applicable procedures
3. (21 CFR 820.25(b))[75] In the event of gaps in fulfillment of competency requirements for an individual, training, or other actions shall be carried out to fill the need.
4. (21 CFR 820.25(b))[76] Records shall be maintained of education, training, skills, and experience for individuals carrying out QMS activities, including temporary and part-time employees.

---

[73] See also ISO 13485, 6.2 for both 1. and 2.

[74] Although 820.25(a) speaks also of the need for "sufficient personnel," the question of sufficiency is best addressed through management responsibility with regard to provision of resources, so that this procedure can focus on the competence of those personnel.

[75] See also ISO 13485, 6.2 b).

[76] See also ISO 13485, 6.2 e).

## Training

1. (21 CFR 820.25(b))[77] Procedures shall be established to identify training needs for each position, including training in procedures applicable to the position, and to ensure that personnel are trained to perform adequately their assigned responsibilities.

2. (21 CFR 820.25(a)) and (21 CFR 820.70(d))[78] Training requirements for individuals carrying out QMS activities shall be fulfilled and documented prior to execution of those activities. However, maintenance personnel or other individuals working temporarily in special environmental conditions may either be trained for those conditions or may be supervised by a trained person.

3. (ISO 13485, 6.2 c)) Assessment of training and other actions taken to ensure competency shall be carried out, including:
   - Assessment of effectiveness of specific training for individuals[79]
   - Overall assessment of the program in place to ensure competency

4. (ISO 13485, 6.2 d)) Department managers shall ensure personnel are aware of the significance of their activities and their contribution to achieving quality objectives. This awareness training shall be documented.

5. (21 CFR 820.25(b)(1)) As part of their training, personnel shall be made aware of product defects which may occur from the improper performance of their specific jobs.

6. (21 CFR 820.25(b)(2)) Personnel who perform verification and validation activities shall be made aware of defects and errors that may be encountered as part of their job functions.

---

[77] See also ISO 13485, 6.2.

[78] See also ISO 13485, 6.4.1 b).

[79] Assessment of effectiveness is quite difficult to ensure in a meaningful way. A quiz on material covered, such as a new or revised procedure, is a practical approach in many cases, but should not be relied upon entirely. Managerial observation and periodic personnel reviews should also address this subject. Furthermore, if the root cause of a large number of CAPA entries is identified as training, the whole approach to training-effectiveness assessment is open to question.

## FACILITIES AND EQUIPMENT

### Responsibilities

*Responsibilities normally are assigned to the departments owning and using the facilities and equipment.*

*The quality or regulatory functions should have responsibility to be involved in approving plans for significant capital expenditures.*

### Requirements

#### Facilities

1. Procedures shall be established to ensure that quality and regulatory concerns are adequately addressed with regard to capital purchases.[80]

2. (21 CFR 820.70(f)) Buildings shall be of suitable design and contain sufficient space to perform necessary operations, prevent mix-ups, and ensure orderly handling.

3. (21 CFR 820.70(c))[81] Where environmental conditions could reasonably be expected to have an adverse effect on product quality, procedures shall be established, such as:

    • To control these environmental conditions adequately
    • To provide for periodic inspections to verify that the system, including necessary equipment, is adequate and functioning properly
    • To ensure that these activities are documented and reviewed.

#### Equipment—General

1. (21 CFR 820.70(a), (g))[82] Equipment used in manufacturing processes shall meet specified requirements, including requirements for monitoring and measurement, and shall be appropriately designed,

---

[80] Although not an explicit requirement of any regulation or standard, it is prudent to ensure that these considerations are part of the capital process on the front end, since it is always more expensive to add them on the back end.

[81] See also ISO 13485, 6.4.1.

[82] See also ISO 13485, 7.6 for both 1. and 5.

constructed, placed, and installed to facilitate maintenance, adjust-ment, cleaning, and use. It shall be approved prior to use.[83]

2. (21 CFR 820.70(g)(1))[84] Schedules shall be established for the adjust-ment, cleaning, and other maintenance of equipment for manufac-turing, work environment, and monitoring/measurement to ensure that specifications are met. Maintenance activities, including the date and individuals performing the maintenance activities, shall be documented.

3. (21 CFR 820.70(g)(2)) Periodic inspections shall be carried out in accordance with established procedures to ensure adherence to applicable equipment maintenance schedules. The inspections, including the date and individuals conducting inspections, shall be documented.

4. (21 CFR 820.70(g)(3)) Inherent limitations or allowable tolerances shall be visibly posted on or near equipment requiring periodic adjustments, or shall be readily available to personnel performing these adjustments. Such postings shall be dated and shall indicate the authorization for the posting.

5. (21 CFR 820.70(i)) Software related to use of equipment shall be validated (ISO 13485, 7.6), *with extent of validation proportionate to associated risk.* See Level 2 software and process validation example.


### Inspection, Measuring, and Test Equipment

1. (21 CFR 820.72(a))[85] Documentation for inspection, measuring, and test equipment, including mechanical, automated, or electronic inspection and test equipment, shall include information showing that it is suitable for its intended purposes and is capable of produc-ing valid results.

2. (21 CFR 820.70(g), 820.72(a)) Procedures shall be established to ensure:
   • That equipment is calibrated or verified at established intervals or prior to use
   • That equipment is inspected, checked and maintained
   • (ISO 13485, 7.6 b), d)) That equipment is adjusted when necessary but also safeguarded from harmful adjustments

---

[83] This sentence is not explicitly required by regulation or quality standards.
[84] See also ISO 13485, 6.3.
[85] See also ISO 13485, 7.6 for 1., 2., and 3.

- That equipment is handled, preserved, and stored so that accuracy and fitness for use are maintained
- That activities required by these procedures are documented

3. (21 CFR 820.72(b)) Calibration procedures shall include:
   - Specific directions and limits for accuracy and precision
   - Provisions for action when accuracy and precision limits are not met: remedial action to reestablish the limits and evaluation whether there was any adverse effect on product quality
   - Requirements for review of results when calibration is outsourced[86]
   - Requirements for documentation of these activities

4. (21 CFR 820.72(b)(1))[87] Calibration standards used for inspection, measuring, and test equipment shall be chosen in the following order of preference:
   a. Traceable to national or international standards
   b. An independent reproducible standard if national or international standards are not practical or available
   c. An established in-house standard if no applicable external standard exists

5. (21 CFR 820.72(b)(2))[88] Equipment identification, calibration dates, the individual performing the calibration, and the next calibration date shall be documented. These records shall be displayed on or near each piece of equipment or shall be readily available to the personnel using such equipment and to the individual(s) responsible for calibrating the equipment.

## SOFTWARE AND PROCESS VALIDATION

### Responsibilities

*Research and development should be responsible for validation of software used in products. For nonproduct software related to the QMS, production, and service, the department having the software installed should be responsible for the validation. (It is also prudent for business reasons to*

---

[86] Not an explicit requirement of a standard or regulation, but frequently checked by third-party auditors.
[87] See also ISO 13485, 7.6 a).
[88] See also ISO 13485, 7.6 c).

*require some level of validation of software even when not related to QMS requirements.)*

*Manufacturing is a logical choice for primary responsibility in process validation, although in some companies this responsibility falls to the quality function. For products in development it may be appropriate to assign responsibility to research and development for the process validation.*

## Requirements

### Software Validation

1. (21 CFR 820.70(i))[89] Documented processes shall be established for validation of software used for products, for the QMS and for production and service. (ISO 13485, 4.1.4, 7.5.6) *Extent of validation shall be proportionate to the risks involved.*
2. (21 CFR 820.30(g)) Validation of software used for product shall be included in design validation and carried out according to the established process.
3. (21 CFR 820.70(i))[90] Software used for production, for monitoring, and for measurement, or the QMS shall be validated for its intended use according to the established process prior to its implementation. Reconfirmation of the validation shall be carried out as necessary.
4. (21 CFR 820.70(i)) Changes to software used for production, for monitoring, and for measurement, or the QMS shall be validated prior to approval and implementation.
5. (21 CFR 820.70(i)) Software validation activities and results shall be documented.

### Process Validation

1. (21 CFR 820.75(a))[91] Where the results of a process cannot be fully verified by subsequent inspection and test, particularly where deficiencies appear only in use of the product or service, the process shall be validated with a high degree of assurance and approved according to established procedures.

---

[89] See also ISO 13485, 7.5.6.
[90] See also ISO 13485, 7.6.
[91] See also ISO 13485, 7.5.6 for 1., 2., 3., 6., and 8.

2. (21 CFR 820.3(z)(2) Validation shall establish by objective evidence that a validated process consistently produces a result or product meeting its predetermined specifications.

3. (21 CFR 820.75) and (GHTF Process Validation Guidance[92]) Establish procedures for process validation that include:
   - Methods defined prior to execution of the validation study
   - Approval criteria defined prior to execution of the study
   - Statistical rationale for sampling plans
   - Provision for equipment approval

4. (21 CFR 820.75(a)) The validation activities and results including the date and signature of the individual(s) approving the validation and where appropriate the major equipment validated, shall be documented.

5. (21 CFR 820.75(b)) Procedures shall be established for monitoring and control of process parameters for validated processes to ensure that the specified requirements continue to be met.

6. (21 CFR 820.75(b)(1)) Established procedures shall ensure that validated processes are performed by qualified individuals.

7. (21 CFR 820.75(b)(2)) For validated processes, the monitoring and control methods and data, the date performed, and, where appropriate, the individuals performing the process or the major equipment used shall be documented.

8. (21 CFR 820.75(b)(3)) and (ISO 13485, 7.5.6 f)) When changes or process deviations occur, the process shall be reviewed and evaluated and revalidation *performed according to defined criteria*. Periodic revalidation shall be required when appropriate even in the absence of changes or deviations. These activities shall be documented.

## DESIGN CONTROL

### Responsibilities

*Primary responsibility for design control is often assigned to the research and development department, although the quality department and other*

---

[92] "Quality Management Systems: Process Validation Guidance," GHTF Guidance SG3/N99-10, January 2004. This GHTF guidance document has been adopted by the FDA as the current guidance for process validation for medical devices.

departments responsible for the product on the market should have defined responsibilities. Because new product development is a multidisciplinary activity, not necessarily owned by research and development, in some cases there may be a separate project management department that owns the new product development process (design control) to reinforce a holistic approach.

## Requirements

### General[93]

1. (21 CFR 820.30(a)(1))[94] Established procedures shall ensure that product design is planned and controlled to ensure that specified design requirements are met.[95]

### Design and Development Planning[96]

1. (21 CFR 820.30(b)) Plans shall be established that describe or reference design and development activities and define the responsibility and authority for implementation. (ISO 13485, 7.3.2 f)) *Plans shall include required competence of personnel.*
2. (21 CFR 820.30(b))[97] Plans shall include:
   - Determination of design and development stages.[98]
   - Activities planned for verification, validation, transfer of the design to manufacturing and review(s) at each stage, postmarket clinical follow-up studies where required,[99] and clear identification of responsibilities for these activities.

---

[93] In the event that ISO 13485 section 7.3 is a permitted exclusion, particular attention must nevertheless be given to fulfillment of the requirements of sections 7.1 and 7.2.

[94] See also ISO 13485, 7.3.1, 7.3.2.

[95] Although certain products may be exempt from design control requirements in certain regulatory jurisdictions, it is prudent to implement design control requirements for all products, scaling the effort, as appropriate, to the level of product risk. Even a company with a site producing only Class 1 products exempt from design control and selling those products only in the United States should choose the discipline of design control because it leads to better products.

[96] In the product-development process, it is normal to plan for both product and project risk. Since project risk is essentially business-related, it is prudent to keep the documentation for project risk separable from the design control documentation subject to external audit.

[97] See also ISO 13485, 7.3.2 for both 2. and 3.

[98] Rather than determine this separately for each development project, it is normal to establish a general process for controlling the design and development of all products, and then to use the plan for each project to scale the activities required for the particular product.

[99] Although technically not part of design control, planning for these studies, if required, should take place during product development.

- Identification and description of interfaces between responsible groups, together with plans for effective communication and assignment of responsibility between groups.[100]
- (ISO 13485, 7.3.2 e)) *Identification of method for traceability of design output back into design input.*

3. (21 CFR 820.30(b)) Plans shall be reviewed, updated, and approved as the design evolves.

### Design Input

1. (21 CFR 820.30(c)) Design input requirements shall be determined for each product that are appropriate and that address the intended use of the product, including needs of the user and the patient. (ISO 13485, 7.3.3) *These requirements shall be capable of verification or validation.*

2. (ISO 13485, 7.2.1, 7.3.3) Design input requirements shall include:
   - Customer requirements for function, usability, and performance, both expressed and not expressed but necessary
   - Regulatory, legal, and safety requirements
   - Any required user training for proper and safe use of the product
   - Internally available information, including (1) information from previous similar designs when available (such as complaints and other customer feedback), (2) risk management information, (3) requirements essential for development, and (4) other internal requirements

3. (21 CFR 820.30(c))[101] Incomplete, ambiguous, or conflicting requirements shall be addressed.[102]

4. (21 CFR 820.30(c)) The design input requirements shall be documented and shall be reviewed and approved by [individual(s) identified by position in the company]. The approval, including the date and signature of the individual(s) approving the requirements, shall be documented.

---

[100] This is particularly important when all or part of the product development or manufacturing is outsourced.

[101] See also ISO 13485, 7.3.3 for both 3 and 4.

[102] The particular process to be followed to address such conflicts and ambiguities must be spelled out in a company procedure. If the process can be succinctly stated (which is likely), it may be appropriate to include its details in this Level 2 design control procedure.

5. Changes to the design input requirements shall be documented as needed during development and shall be approved at the same level as the original requirements.[103]

6. (21 CFR 820.30(j)) Design input shall be documented in the design history file.

## Design Output

1. (21 CFR 820.30(d))[104] Design output shall meet input requirements and shall be defined and documented in a manner that allows an adequate evaluation of its ability to meet design input requirements.

2. (21 CFR 820.30(d))[105] Design output shall contain or make reference to acceptance criteria.

3. (21 CFR 820.3(g))[106] Design output shall include the product, its packaging and labeling, and its device master record (DMR) (including, but not limited to, information needed for purchasing, production, and service).

4. (21 CFR 820.30(d))[107] Design output shall include identification of the outputs that are essential for the proper functioning of the product.

5. (21 CFR 820.30(d)) The design output shall be documented and shall be reviewed and approved by [individual(s) identified by position in the company] before release.[108] The approval, including the date and signature of the individual(s) approving the output, shall be documented.

6. (21 CFR 820.30(j)) Design output shall be documented in the design history file.[109]

---

[103] The approval level is not explicitly stated, but clearly expected by authorities.

[104] See also ISO 13485, 7.3.4.

[105] See also ISO 13485, 7.3.4 c).

[106] See also ISO 13485, 7.3.4 b).

[107] See also ISO 13485, 7.3.4 d).

[108] An efficient approach to handle this approval is to document that the final design review approval (by signature and date) constitutes the approval for the components of the design output. Some companies choose to make the signature approval for design output components be the approval of each component of the DMR.

[109] Note that ultimate documentation for studies supporting the design output is normally a collection of laboratory notebooks. This does not mean that laboratory notebooks need to be part of the design output or the design history file. However, it does mean that there needs to be a documented trail of evidence from reports and other documents leading back to the laboratory notebooks. Although it is unlikely that an investigator will pursue this trail, it is possible and should be planned for.

## Design Review

1. (21 CFR 820.30(e))[110] A design review shall be planned, conducted and documented at each stage of product development applicable to the product to determine the ability of the design to meet requirements. If scaling of the development process leads to omission of a particular stage, then the requirements of the design review for that stage shall be addressed by the time of the design review for the subsequent stage.
2. (21 CFR 820.30(e)) Participants at each design review shall include:
   • Representatives of all functions concerned with the design stage being reviewed
   • At least one individual who does not have direct responsibility for the design stage being reviewed
   • Any specialists needed
3. (ISO 13485, 7.3.5 b)) The review shall identify any problems with the design and actions to be taken to resolve those problems.[111]
4. The review shall include risk management considerations appropriate to the design stage. The final design review prior to market entry shall consider the overall residual risk and shall determine that this risk is acceptable if the product is to be marketed.[112]
5. (21 CFR 820.30(e))[113] The results of each design review, including identification of the design, the date, and the individual(s) performing the review shall be documented in the design history file.

## Design Verification

1. (21 CFR 820.30(f))[114] Design verification shall confirm that the design output meets the design input requirements.[115]
2. (ISO 13485, 7.3.6) *Verification plans shall include methods to be used, criteria for acceptance, and statistical rationale for sample size(s).*

---

[110] See also ISO 13485, 7.3.5 for 1., 2., and 5.
[111] This does not mean that solutions must be identified at the review.
[112] This sentence is intended to ensure documentation of fulfillment of the requirements of ISO 14971.
[113] See also ISO 13485, 7.3.5.
[114] See also ISO 13485, 7.3.6 for both 1. and 2.
[115] Normally this is done by translating requirements into detailed specifications and then verifying by test that each specification has been verified.

*Where the product is intended to function connected/interfaced to another product, verification shall include testing of the connection(s).*

3. (21 CFR 820.30(f)) The results of the design verification, including the verification of the design, methods, the date, and individuals performing verification, shall be documented in the design history file.

### Design Validation

1. (21 CFR 820.30(g))[116] Design validation shall ensure products conform to defined user needs and intended uses and shall include testing of production units under actual or simulated use conditions, such as a clinical evaluation or other evaluation of performance.

2. (21 CFR 820.30(g)) and (ISO 13485, 7.3.7) Design validation shall be carried out prior to placing a product on the market.

3. (21 CFR 820.30(g)) Design validation shall be performed under defined operating conditions on initial production units, lots, or batches, or their equivalents.

4. (ISO 13485, 7.3.7) *Validation plans shall include methods to be used, criteria for acceptance, and statistical rationale for sample size(s). Where the product is intended to function connected/interfaced to another product, validation shall include testing of the connection(s).*

5. (21 CFR 820.30(g)) Design validation shall include software validation for products containing or otherwise requiring software.

6. (21 CFR 820.30(g)) Design validation shall include risk management considerations.

7. When clinical investigations are carried out for purposes of design validation, these investigations shall be in compliance with regulations established in the country/region where the investigation is being carried out.[117]

---

[116] See also ISO 13485, 7.3.7 for both 1. and 7.

[117] Although this statement appears self-evident, it is useful as a reminder that there are (quite appropriately) a large number of regulations applicable to clinical investigations in each country/region. Companies conducting clinical investigations should have a number of Level 3 procedures in place that ensure compliance with regulations wherever the investigations are conducted. Companies outsourcing clinical investigations must ensure that supplier evaluations of the service provider address this subject.

8. (21 CFR 820.30(g)) The results of the design validation, including identification of the design, methods, the date, and the individuals performing the validation, shall be documented in the design history file.

### Design Transfer

1. (21 CFR 820.30(h))[118] The product design shall be correctly translated into production specifications as documented in the device master record.
2. The risks associated with the production process shall be documented and addressed.[119]
3. Where appropriate, production processes shall be validated. (See Level 2 example: Software and process validation.)

### Design Changes[120]

1. (21 CFR 820.30(i))[121] Each design change shall be assessed for the risks associated with the change and to ensure that the change does not introduce new risks. The level of verification and, if needed, validation testing, should be in relation to the risks identified.
2. (21 CFR 820.30(i)) Each design change shall be verified.
3. (21 CFR 820.30(i)) Each design change that has potential to change the established design input requirements shall be validated.
4. (21 CFR 820.30(i)) Design changes shall be reviewed and approved prior to their implementation.
   - Design changes during development shall be approved at the design review prior to completion of design transfer.
   - (ISO 13485, 7.3.9) After transfer of the design to production, design changes shall be reviewed and approved in accordance

---

[118] See also ISO 13485, 7.3.8.

[119] This statement is intended to address fulfillment of requirements of ISO 14971.

[120] Design changes during development are straightforward so long as no changes are implemented after design validation or after regulatory marketing approvals. Changes once the product is in production, although in principle subject to all the same considerations, are more complex and can have more ramifications. Thus change control in production deserves particular attention: see Level 2 example "Change Control." If changes are made during development after design validation or regulatory marketing approval, these changes should be reviewed as for product in production.

[121] See also ISO 13485, 7.3.9 for 1., 2., 3., and 4.

with applicable requirements for change during production. The review of changes in production shall include the possible effect of the changes on product already delivered, as well as parts/materials for these products. See Level 2 example for Change Control.

5. (21 CFR 820.30(j)) and (21 CFR 820.70(b)) Design changes shall be documented. During development, design changes shall be documented in the design history file (DHF). During production, design changes shall be documented in the device master record (DMR).[122]

## *Design History File*

1. 21 CFR 820.30(j).[123] The design history file (DHF) shall contain or reference the records necessary to demonstrate that the design was developed in accordance with this procedure, and therefore in accordance with applicable regulations and standards.

2. The approval, including the date and signature of the individual(s) approving the design history file, shall be documented.[124]

3. The design history file shall contain or reference the risk management file.

4. The design history file shall contain or reference any required post-market clinical follow-up evaluation report, or documented justification for why a postmarket clinical follow-up investigation is not necessary.[125]

---

[122] This statement implies that the design history file is completed and closed at the conclusion of the development process, with the possible exception of the inclusion of any required postmarket clinical follow-up report. Sections of the design history file needed to maintain the product during its lifetime (such as the risk management file) are incorporated in the device master record, and are used to manage change control within the device master record for the life of the product.

   An alternative, entirely acceptable, approach is to maintain the design history file as a living document throughout the lifetime of the product. For most companies, this is more cumbersome.

[123] See also ISO 13485, 7.3.10.

[124] If product is not to be sold in South America, this requirement may be omitted. See Chapter 5.

[125] Although not strictly part of design control, these studies and the resulting report have a logical home as part of the design history file. If a company does not specify that this documentation is to be part of the design history file, then it should probably specify it as part of the device master record. This study (or the justification for not conducting it) is a critical component of required technical documentation for Europe.

---

## SUPPLIER QUALITY MANAGEMENT

### Responsibilities

*Responsibilities in this area are shared among the quality department, the purchasing department, and in the qualification of new suppliers, the research and development department or, possibly, the manufacturing department, for products already in production. The regulatory department should be responsible for questions related to registration requirements for the supplier.*

### Requirements

#### General[126]

1. (21 CFR 820.50)[127] Procedures shall be established to ensure that all purchased or otherwise received products and services conform to specified requirements.
2. (21 CFR 820.50(a))[128] Requirements, including quality requirements, that must be met by suppliers, contractors, and consultants shall be established.[129]
3. Critical suppliers should be made aware of the (remote) possibility that they may be subject to unannounced audits by a notified body.[130]

#### Supplier Evaluation

1. (21 CFR 820.50(a)(1)) and (ISO 13485, 7.4.1) Potential suppliers, contractors, and consultants shall be evaluated and selected on the basis of the following:
   - Their ability to meet specified requirements, including quality requirements

---

[126] There is an excellent flowchart for supplier quality management in "ISO 13485:2016, Medical devices: A practical guide."

[127] See also ISO 13485, 7.4.1.

[128] See also ISO 13485, 7.4.1.

[129] Note that this requirement applies not just to other companies but also to sources of materials or services within the same company but outside the scope of the QMS.

[130] Unannounced audits are a relatively new concept for notified bodies and the likelihood of unannounced audits of critical suppliers is not yet clear. Given resources available for unannounced audits in general, unannounced audits of most suppliers seem improbable. However, a company would not want a critical supplier to be completely surprised by such an event.

- The effect(s) of the purchased material on the finished product
- *The level of risk associated with the product*

The evaluation shall be documented, including required actions arising from the evaluation.

2. During product development, a supplier development team should be established when appropriate.[131]
   - Evaluations should qualify material suppliers for specific supplier sites and equipment.[132] Normally, it is most efficient for research and development to work with suppliers that are already approved for the type of material needed, so that assessment of the supplier is more efficient.[133]
   - For suppliers that carry out development or codevelopment, supplier approval should be completed prior to an early design review. If such approval is not complete by the expected review, the review shall include explicit consideration of the resulting risk to the project and to the product under development.
   - For all suppliers, supplier approval shall be completed by the design review prior to design validation.

### Supplier Maintenance

1. (21 CFR 820.50(a)(2) and related Preamble, Section 99.[134] The type and extent of control to be exercised over the product, services, suppliers, contractors, and consultants, including criteria for re-evaluation, shall be based on the following:
   - The results of the evaluations conducted
   - The risks associated with the purchased material or services for finished product[135]

---

[131] This item is not explicitly required by quality standards or regulation.

[132] It is not enough to verify that a supplier is on the approved/evaluated supplier list. The supplier may be on the list for material made at a different site or on different equipment with a different process.

[133] Some companies may wish to strengthen this statement to require research and development to use current suppliers unless there is a strong rationale to qualify a new supplier.

[134] See also ISO 13485, 7.4.1.

[135] It would be appropriate to summarize or reference at this point in the procedure a tiered system for supplier classification.

2. Supplier maintenance processes shall ensure ongoing satisfactory fulfillment of requirements.
   - Suppliers shall be evaluated continually through combinations of incoming inspection results, delivery performance, QMS assessments, and CAPA reports.
   - (ISO 13485, 7.4.1) *Issues with suppliers shall be addressed in a manner proportionate to the risks involved.*
   - Where necessary, corrective actions with suppliers shall be initiated and supplier disqualification shall be considered as an option when necessary.

### Supplier Disqualification[136]

1. Suppliers of materials or services, or specific parts, materials, or services from a supplier, may be disqualified after attempts at corrective action have proved ineffective. Disqualification may be related to, but not limited to:
   - Quality
   - Price
   - Delivery
   - Service
   Note: Where contractual arrangements are involved, legal advice should normally be part of the process.[137]
2. Disqualifications shall be documented.
3. Pending disqualification, steps shall be taken to limit or prevent receipt of material from the supplier where appropriate.
4. Disqualification of a supplier for one part or material may not affect other parts or material from the same supplier.

### Outsourced Processes

1. (21 CFR 820.50 and related Preamble, Section 100)[138] Outsourced processes are QMS services and shall be identified and controlled. Consideration shall be given to the ability of the supplier/provider

---

[136] Although not explicitly required by regulation or standard, authorities expect to find provisions for disqualification of suppliers. Auditors are likely to ask for examples.

[137] Many companies will wish to make this provision stronger, to require consultation with the legal department. It is possible for disqualification activities to cause legal problems even when the supplier is perceived as the party at fault.

[138] See also ISO 13485, 4.1.5.

to meet regulatory/legal requirements applicable to the product or service supplied. (ISO 13485, 4.1.5) *The extent of control shall be based on the possible risks for products and the QMS; a written quality agreement is required.*

2. (21 CFR 820.50 and related Preamble, Section 100) Original equipment manufacturers (OEMs), contract manufacturers, and suppliers of external services, including external development services shall be evaluated to ensure that supplied products and the QMS of the supplier consistently meet specified requirements. Particular attention shall be given to fulfillment of regulatory/legal requirements.[139]

3. A determination shall be made whether a contractor is required to be a Registered Device Manufacturer. In the case of software development, a determination shall be made whether the software is a medical device and whether the service provider is required to be a Registered Device Manufacturer.

4. For OEMs, contract manufacturers and suppliers of external development services, a contract is required.[140] Exceptions require documented rationale and regulatory approval. The contract shall include provisions for quality and regulatory requirements, and, as applicable, provisions for:
   - Responsibility for product registration
   - Responsibility for service/support
   - Responsibility for customer complaints
   - Responsibility for corrective actions for product released to market

### Purchasing Information/Records

1. (21 CFR 820.50(a)(3)) Records of acceptable suppliers, contractors, and consultants shall be established and maintained. A list of evaluated suppliers should be established.[141]

---

[139] To a degree this duplicates requirements elsewhere in this procedure, but this area often deserves extra emphasis.

[140] Not a requirement of a regulation or standard.

[141] Not an explicit requirement of a regulation or standard, but a common and extremely useful practice. Although some companies maintain an approved supplier list, it is important to provide colleagues with information about suppliers that have been evaluated but have not been approved. An evaluated supplier list is more useful.

2. (21 CFR 820.50(b) and Preamble, Section 99)[142] Data to describe clearly or reference specified requirements shall be established and maintained for purchased or otherwise received product and services. These data shall include quality requirements as appropriate, such as QMS requirements, product requirements, process requirements, testing requirements at the supplier, and personnel qualification requirements.[143]

3. (ISO 13485, 7.4.2) The adequacy of purchasing data describing requirements shall be determined prior to communication of these requirements to the supplier.

4. (21 CFR 820.50(b)) Purchasing data shall be approved by signature and date.

5. (21 CFR 820.50(b))[144] Purchasing documents shall include, where possible, an agreement that the suppliers, contractors, and consultants agree to provide notification of changes in the product or service so that the company may determine whether the changes may affect the quality of the finished product.

6. (ISO 13485, 7.4.2) To the extent required by established requirements for traceability, purchasing documentation, and records shall be established and maintained.

## PRODUCT REGULATORY COMPLIANCE[145]

### Responsibilities

*Most of the requirements in this area should be assigned to the regulatory function. To the extent this function is outsourced, these responsibilities*

---

[142] See also ISO 13485, 7.4.2, 7.4.3.

[143] Note that these are items that must be assessed in the original supplier assessment as well as during supplier maintenance.

[144] See also ISO 13485, 7.4.2.

[145] Although requirements for quality management systems are not subject to frequent changes, the product regulatory arena is one in which detailed requirements can be expected to change on almost a yearly basis in one country/region or another. What is important for each company is the identification of key regulatory areas affecting their products.

   In each product regulatory area it is important to document in a company procedure the details of how regulatory requirements are to be met in all markets where products are made available. It would be inappropriate to assume that fulfilling FDA expectations will meet all requirements for regulatory actions around the world. It would also be inefficient to require regulatory staff to refer to the regulations of each country or region each time they must execute regulatory requirements around the world.

*should be managed by available regulatory resources, together with the quality and research and development functions if necessary, through supplier quality management.*

## Requirements

### General

1. Procedure(s) shall be established to cover the strategy for regulatory compliance, including processes for identification of relevant legal requirements, qualification, classification, handling of equivalence, choice of and compliance with conformity assessment procedures.[146]
2. Processes shall be established to ensure that questions and issues raised by regulatory authorities are handled effectively.
3. The establishment of positions with specified responsibilities where required by regulation[147] shall be documented.
4. (ISO 13485, 7.2.3) *Communication with regulatory authorities shall take place as required by applicable regulations.*[148]
5. Company representatives geographically located where products are marketed shall be established where required by regulatory authorities.
6. A contract with a notified body shall address requirements. In case of change of notified body, a contract with both notified bodies shall address requirements related to the change.[149]
7. Processes shall be established to ensure that changes in regulatory requirements affecting the company are identified in a timely manner.

---

[146] Although this is strictly a requirement from MDR, Annex IX, Chapter I, and IVDR, Annex IX, Chapter I, ISO 13485:2016 also requires the QMS to ensure that all applicable regulatory requirements are met. This means there must be objective evidence of compliance with regulations in any markets where products are sold.

[147] This provision addresses the provision in new European regulations requiring "qualified persons" with responsibilities specified in the regulation. It also addresses the requirement for an authorized representative if the manufacturer is not established in a member state of the European Union. In each case, a Level 2 procedure for a company should elaborate on the requirements in more detail.

[148] Although this provision is self-evident, it is prudent to include this statement in company documentation because third party auditors may expect to see evidence that this addition to ISO 13485 has been incorporated into the QMS.

[149] Although this might under normal circumstances be an improbable event, with the increased scrutiny of notified bodies together with the anticipated reduction in number of notified bodies in Europe, it may occur with increased frequency in coming years. This requirement is addressed specifically in the new European medical device regulations, and thus it is advisable to document in a company procedure.

### Marketing Authorization

1. Processes shall be established to ensure that marketing approval requirements for each type/class of product for each intended market are identified early in the development process and are monitored through the development process to identify any changes in those requirements.
2. Processes shall be established to ensure that product re-registration requirements are maintained up to date and that re-registrations are executed in a timely manner.
3. (ISO 13485, 4.1.1) *Processes shall be established to ensure that there is objective evidence of competence with regulatory requirements for all jurisdictions where products are marketed.*

### Product Labeling and Identification

1. Processes shall be established to ensure that labeling requirements are met.
2. Processes shall be established to ensure that product identification requirements (Unique Device Identification [UDI]) are met in applicable markets.

### Combination Products

1. Particular attention shall be given to QMS requirements for device/drug or device/biological combination products. Required details shall be added to established processes; any additional required processes shall be established.[150]

---

## PRODUCTION

### Responsibilities

*Primary responsibilities in this area are assigned to the manufacturing function. To the extent this function is outsourced these responsibilities should be managed by available manufacturing resources and the quality function through supplier quality management.*

---

[150] See Appendix A, Table A-1, for an indication of the gaps between drug and device regulations in the United States. Similar information will be required for markets outside the United States.

*It may be appropriate to assign responsibility for some activities (such as product documentation and/or labeling) to the quality department.*

## Requirements

### General

1. (21 CFR 820.70(a))[151] Production processes shall be developed, conducted, controlled, and monitored to ensure that products conform to specifications.
2. (21 CFR 820.70(a)) Where deviations from product specifications could occur as a result of the manufacturing process, process control procedures shall be established that describe any process controls necessary to assure conformance to specifications.
3. Where process controls are needed, they shall include:
   - (21 CFR 820.70(a)(1)) Documented instructions, standard operating procedures, and methods that define and control the manner of production
   - (21 CFR 820.70(a)(2)) Monitoring and control of process parameters and component and product characteristics during production
   - (21 CFR 820.70(a)(3)) Compliance with specified reference standards or codes
   - (21 CFR 820.70(a)(4)) The approval of processes and process equipment (see also Level 2 example for Facilities and Equipment)
   - (21 CFR 820.70(a)(5)) Criteria for workmanship expressed in documented standards or by means of identified and approved representative samples.
4. If instructions are posted near equipment, the authorization for the posting and the date of the posting shall be clear.[152]

---

[151] See also ISO 13485, 7.5.1.

[152] Although not explicitly required by regulation or standard, this level of attention to postings is necessary to assure no unauthorized postings.

### Production and Process Changes[153]

1. (21 CFR 820.70(b)) Procedures shall be established for changes to a specification, method, process, or procedure.
2. (21 CFR 820.70(b)) Such changes shall be verified and, where appropriate, also validated before implementation.
3. (21 CFR 820.70(b)) Change documentation shall be reviewed for adequacy and approved prior to implementation by signature and date of the individuals designated to approve the change.
4. (21 CFR 820.70(b)) These activities shall be documented.

### Identification and Traceability

1. (21 CFR 820.60, 820.90)[154] Procedures shall be established to ensure that:
   - Product is properly identified throughout the production process, from receipt through to distribution and, where appropriate, installation.
   - (ISO 13485, 7.5.8) *Product is assigned a unique device identification if required by regulation.*
   - Returned product is identified separately and treated as potentially nonconforming product until after a formal documented evaluation.
2. (21 CFR 820.60 and Preamble, Section 117)[155] Procedures shall be established to ensure that traceability requirements for materials and products are determined and documented.
3. (21 CFR 820.65, 820.120(e))[156] In the case of:
   - Products intended for surgical implant into the body
   - Products intended to support or sustain life and whose failure to perform when properly used can be reasonably expected to result in a significant injury to the user
   - Other products identified by a regulatory authority as requiring traceability

---

[153] See also Level 2 provisions related to design change under design control, as well as the Level 2 example for change control. These must all be consistent with each other. One way of ensuring this could be to have pointers from the change sections of the design control and production Level 2 procedures to the Level 2 change control procedure, which would then cover all aspects of change control.

[154] See also ISO 13485, 7.5.8.

[155] See also ISO 13485, 7.5.9.1.

[156] See also ISO 13485, 7.5.9.1, 7.5.9.2.

procedures shall be established for identifying with a control number each unit, lot, or batch of finished products and for ensuring that the control number accompanies the product through distribution.[157]

Records shall also be maintained of components, materials and production environmental conditions if these factors could cause product malfunction. The procedures shall facilitate corrective action. This documentation shall be included in the device history record (DHR). (See below under Product Documentation.)

### Status

1. (21 CFR 820.86)[158] Procedures shall be established to ensure the following:
   - That the acceptance status of product is identified by suitable means, to indicate the conformance or nonconformance of product with acceptance criteria
   - That the identification of acceptance status is maintained throughout manufacturing, packaging, labeling, installation, and servicing of the product to ensure that only product which has passed the required acceptance activities is distributed, used, or installed

### Cleanliness

1. (21 CFR 820.70(e))[159] Procedures shall be established to prevent contamination of equipment or product by substances that could reasonably be expected to have an adverse effect on product quality. These procedures shall include provision for validation of cleaning processes where needed.[160] Where appropriate, these procedures shall address regulatory requirements for employee safety and the environment.
2. (21 CFR 820.70(h))[161] Where a manufacturing material could reasonably be expected to have an adverse effect on product quality,

---

[157] Depending upon the type of products sold by the company, this provision may not be needed.

[158] See also ISO 13485, 7.5.8.

[159] See also ISO 13485, 6.4.2, 7.5.2 a), b), c), d).

[160] See Global Harmonization Task Force (GHTF) guidance on process validation. This guidance document has been adopted by the FDA as appropriate guidance on process validation for medical devices.

[161] See also ISO 13485, 7.5.2 e).

procedures shall be established to ensure that it is removed or limited to an amount that does not adversely affect product quality, and that the removal or limitation is documented.

3. (21 CFR 820.70(d))[162] Procedures shall establish requirements for the health, cleanliness, personal practices, and clothing of personnel if contact between such personnel and product or environment could reasonably be expected to have an adverse effect on product quality.

### Sterilization

1. (21 CFR 820.70(b) and Preamble, Section 125)[163] Procedures shall be established to ensure validation of sterilization processes prior to their use in product manufacture. Records of this validation shall be maintained (See software and process validation).
2. (ISO 13485, 7.5.5) Procedures shall ensure that records of sterilization process parameters traceable to each production lot are maintained.

### Labeling

1. (21 CFR 820.120)[164] Procedures shall be established to control labeling activities.
2. (21 CFR 820.120(a)) Labels shall be printed and applied so as to remain legible and affixed during the customary conditions of processing, storage, handling, distribution, and, where appropriate, use.
3. (21 CFR 820.120(c)) Established procedures shall ensure that labeling is stored in a manner that provides proper identification and is designed to prevent mix-ups.
4. (21 CFR 820.120(d)) Established procedures for labeling and packaging operations shall ensure sufficient control to prevent labeling mix-ups.
5. (21 CFR 820.120(d)) The label and labeling used for each production unit, lot, or batch shall be documented in the device history record (see below under "Production Documentation").

---

[162] See also ISO 13485, 6.4.1 a).
[163] See also ISO 13485, 7.5.7.
[164] See also ISO 13485, 7.5.1 e).

## Customer Property

1. (21 CFR 820.50 and Preamble, Section 100) and (ISO 13485, 7.5.10) In the event that property of a customer, including intellectual property or other confidential information, comes under control of the company, it shall receive care in accordance with practices for material received from other sources. Procedures shall ensure that it is identified and safeguarded.
2. (ISO 13485, 7.5.10) If customer property becomes adversely affected, procedures shall ensure that the customer is notified and records of the incident are maintained.

## Production Documentation

1. (21 CFR 820.181) For each product, a Device Master Record (DMR) shall be prepared, reviewed for accuracy and approved prior to implementation by signature and date of individuals designated in established procedures.
2. (21 CFR 820.181)[165] The DMR for each type of product shall include, or refer to the location of, the following information:
   - (21 CFR 820.181(a)) Product specifications including appropriate drawings, composition, formulation, component specifications, and software specifications
   - (21 CFR 820.181(b)) Production process specifications including the appropriate equipment specifications, production methods, production procedures, and production environment specification
   - (21 CFR 820.181(c)) Quality assurance procedures and specifications including acceptance criteria and the quality assurance equipment to be used
   - (21 CFR 820.181(d)) Packaging and labeling specifications, including methods and processes used
   - (21 CFR 820.181(e)) Installation, maintenance, and servicing procedures and methods
3. (MDR, Annex II; IVDR, Annex II) The technical documentation and, if applicable, the summary thereof, shall be presented in a clear, organized, readily searchable, and unambiguous manner and

---

[165] See also ISO 13485, 4.2.3, 7.5.1.

shall include the elements of Annex II of the applicable European regulation.[166]

4. (MDR, Annex III; IVDR, Annex III) The technical documentation on postmarket surveillance shall be presented in a clear, organized, readily searchable, and unambiguous manner and shall include the elements of Annex III of the applicable European regulation.[167]

5. (21 CFR 820.184) Procedures shall be established to ensure that device history records for each [batch, lot, or unit—insert appropriate company term(s)] are maintained that demonstrate the product has been manufactured in accordance with the DMR and other QMS requirements.

6. (21 CFR 820.184)[168] The DHR shall include or refer to the location of, the following information:

- (21 CFR 820.184(a)) The dates of manufacture
- (21 CFR 820.184(b)) The quantity manufactured
- (21 CFR 820.184(c)) The quantity released for distribution
- (21 CFR 820.184(d)) The acceptance records that demonstrate the product is manufactured in accordance with the DMR
- (21 CFR 820.184(e)) The primary identification label and labeling used for each production unit
- (21 CFR 820.184(f)) Any product identification(s) and control number(s) used, including traceability documentation where required (see Identification and Traceability section above)
- For sterile products, the records of sterilization process parameters traceable to each batch
- (ISO 13485, 8.2.6) For implantable products, the identity of individuals carrying out inspection or testing

---

[166] The technical documentation for products sold in Europe may not be identical with the DMR. It should be separately identified for each product. If no products are to be sold in Europe, this provision may be eliminated.

[167] If no products are to be sold in Europe, this provision may be eliminated.

[168] See also ISO 13485, 7.5.1.

# CHANGE CONTROL[169]

## Responsibilities

*The manufacturing and quality functions should be responsible for most aspects of change control for marketed products. The regulatory function must be responsible in areas that may affect marketing approvals. The research and development function is often assigned responsibilities related to recently introduced products.*

## Requirements

1. A change control board shall be established to oversee changes in products in production.[170]
2. For each proposed change, the risk management file shall be reviewed to determine the risk(s) associated with the proposed change.[171]
3. For each proposed change, the regulatory approval status of the product shall be considered to determine whether a new application or other regulatory action is required.[172]
4. (21 CFR 820.70(b) and Preamble, Sections 89 and 125) Established processes shall ensure that each change is verified to confirm that specifications and requirements for the product can continue to be met.
5. (21 CFR 820.70(b) and Preamble Sections 89 and 125) If the change is a process change to a validated process, the process shall be revalidated.
6. (21 CFR 820.70(i))[173] If the change involves a change to software, the software shall be revalidated.

---

[169] Note that all of these requirements are already addressed elsewhere in Level 2 documentation. Nevertheless, because of the importance of good change control and the many aspects involved, it can be useful to maintain a separate Level 2 document that brings all the required pieces together. There must be sufficient cross-referencing to ensure that a change in one procedure will require a change in the related procedure(s).

[170] Not explicitly required by quality standard or regulation.

[171] Although not explicitly required by quality standard or regulation, this approach is likely to be the most efficient way to address the requirements of ISO 13485:2016, 7.3.9.

[172] In order not to burden regulatory staff with every product change, a company may wish to document that changes meeting specified criteria indicating a low level of risk/concern do not require formal regulatory review.

[173] See also ISO 13485, 7.5.6.

7. (21 CFR 820.30(i))[174] If the proposed change will result in a change in the design input requirements, the product design shall be revalidated in accordance with design validation requirements.[175, 176]

8. (21 CFR 820.70(b)) Established processes shall ensure that documentation affected by the change can be readily identified and revised to meet new requirements.

9. Verification studies, validation studies where appropriate, an overall assessment of risk(s), and affected documentation shall be reviewed by the change control board. (21 CFR 820.70(b)). Changes shall be approved prior to implementation.

## INSPECTION, TEST, DISPOSITION

### Responsibilities

*Quality is normally responsible for most of the actions covered by this process. Often the manufacturing function has responsibility for some in-process testing.*

### Requirements

#### General

1. (21 CFR 820.60)[177] Procedures shall be established for identifying product during all stages of receipt, production, distribution, and installation to prevent mix-ups.

2. (21 CFR 820.80(a))[178] Procedures shall be established for acceptance activities necessary to ensure product conformance. Acceptance activities include inspections, tests, or other verification activities.

---

[174] See also ISO 13485, 7.3.9.

[175] If the change is not expected to result in a change in design input requirements, but may affect them, the change control board may determine that a design validation study should be carried out in order to assure that no change in performance has taken place.

[176] A company may choose to require that any product improvement project affecting design input requirements must necessarily go through the company's formal design control process. If this is not done, the company must nevertheless ensure fulfillment of design control requirements for design change.

[177] See also ISO 13485, 7.5.8.

[178] See also ISO 13485, 8.1 a).

3. (21 CFR 820.80(e))[179] Acceptance activities shall be documented. Records shall include:
   - The acceptance activities performed
   - The dates acceptance activities are performed
   - The results
   - The signature of the individual(s) conducting the acceptance activities
   - The equipment used as specified in the applicable procedure(s)[180]

   These records shall be part of the device history records.
4. (ISO 13485, 8.2.6) For products that are to be implanted, records shall also include the identity of personnel performing inspection and testing.[181]

### Incoming Acceptance

1. (21 CFR 820.80(b))[182] Procedures shall be established for acceptance of incoming product in order to ensure that materials meet established purchasing requirements.
2. (21 CFR 820.80(b)) Incoming product shall be inspected, tested, or otherwise verified as conforming to specified requirements.
3. (ISO 13485, 7.4.3) *The extent of acceptance testing shall be based on associated risks.*
4. (ISO 13485, 7.4.3) *In the event of changes observed and/or documented regarding incoming product, a determination shall be made whether the changes affect process or product.*
5. (21 CFR 820.80(b) and Preamble, Section 99) Acceptance or rejection shall be documented. Documentation shall include any instances where verification is carried out at a supplier's facility.[183]

---

[179] See also ISO 13485, 7.2.6.

[180] The wording of 820.80(e)(5) is: "where appropriate the equipment used." Although it is appropriate for the FDA to use the phrase "where appropriate," in company procedures it is best to avoid the phrase in order to make clear to all in the company what is expected.

[181] If such products are not in scope of the QMS and the company is unlikely to acquire such products, this provision would normally be omitted.

[182] See also ISO 13485, 7.4.3.

[183] This sentence can be omitted if there are no such instances.

### Labeling Acceptance

1. (21 CFR 820.120(b)) Established procedures shall ensure that labeling is not released for storage or use until a designated individual(s) has examined the labeling for accuracy including, where applicable, the correct expiration date, control number, storage instructions, handling instructions, and any additional processing instructions.
2. (21 CFR 820.120(b)) Established procedures shall ensure that the release, including the date and signature of the individual(s) performing the examination, is documented in the device history record.

### In-Process Acceptance

1. (21 CFR 820.80(c)) Acceptance procedures shall be established for in-process testing and maintained as part of the DMR when determined necessary to ensure that specified requirements for in-process product are met.
2. (21 CFR 820.80(c)) Established procedures shall ensure that in-process product is controlled until the required inspection and test or other verification activities have been completed, or necessary approvals are received, and are documented.

### Final Acceptance

1. (21 CFR 820.80(d))[184] Procedures shall be established for finished product acceptance to ensure that each production [run, lot, or batch—insert appropriate company term(s)] of finished product meets acceptance criteria.
2. (21 CFR 820.80(d)) Established procedures shall ensure that finished product is held in quarantine or otherwise adequately controlled until released.
3. (21 CFR 820.80(d))[185] Finished product shall not be released for distribution until:
   • The activities required in the Device Master Record are completed.
   • The associated data and documentation are reviewed.

---

[184] See also ISO 13485, 7.5.1 f).
[185] See also ISO 13485, 8.2.6.

- The release is authorized by the signature of a designated individual(s).
- The authorization is dated.

### Data Analysis and Statistical Techniques[186]

1. (21 CFR 820.100, 21 CFR 820.250)[187] Procedures shall be established for data collection and valid statistical analysis needed to ensure process and product quality.[188]
2. (21 CFR 820.100) Data to be analyzed shall include data from monitoring and measurement, as well as other relevant data. Of specific importance to be included are:
    - Complaint data and other feedback
    - Product quality data
    - Supplier data
    - Audits
    - Service reports
    - Statistical trends for processes and products, including possibilities for preventive action
3. (21 CFR 820.100) Records of data analysis shall be maintained.
4. (21 CFR 820.250(b)) Sampling plans, when used, shall be written and based on a valid statistical rationale. Procedures shall be established to ensure that sampling methods are adequate for their intended use and to ensure that when changes occur the sampling plans are reviewed. These activities shall be documented.

---

# HANDLING, STORAGE, PRESERVATION, DELIVERY

## Responsibilities

*Definition of responsibilities in this are dependent upon company organization. To the extent these actions are outsourced, responsibilities should be managed through supplier quality management.*

---

[186] It may be desirable to separate the data analysis and statistical techniques section into a separate Level 2 procedure. If this is done, there is applicable advice in "ISO 13485:2016, Medical devices: A practical guide."

[187] See also ISO 13485, 8.4 for 1., 2., and 3.

[188] Ensure coverage of research and development for actions during design control.

## Requirements

### General

1. (21 CFR 820.86) Established procedures shall ensure that acceptance status of product is maintained throughout handling, storage, delivery, installation, and servicing of the product to ensure that only product that has passed the required acceptance activities is distributed, used, or installed.[189]

2. (21 CFR 820.130)[190] Established procedures shall ensure that product packaging and shipping containers are designed and constructed to protect the product from alteration or damage during the customary conditions of processing, storage, handling, and distribution.

### Handling

1. (21 CFR 820.140) Procedures shall be established to ensure that mix-ups, damage, deterioration, contamination, or other adverse effects to product do not occur during handling.

### Storage

1. (21 CFR 820.150(a)) Procedures shall be established for the control of storage areas and stock rooms for product to prevent mix-ups, damage, deterioration, contamination, or other adverse effects pending use or distribution and to ensure that no obsolete, rejected, or deteriorated product is used or distributed.

2. (21CFR820.150(b)) Procedures shall be established to address the methods for authorizing receipt from and dispatch to storage areas and stockrooms.

3. (21 CFR 820.150(a)) When the quality of product deteriorates over time, the product shall be stored in a manner to facilitate proper stock rotation. Where necessary to ensure product quality, procedures shall ensure assessment of its condition.

4. (21 CFR 820.70(c)) When the quality of product requires special storage conditions, established procedures shall ensure that required conditions are maintained.

---

[189] The same subject matter is in the production section, but with a different emphasis.
[190] See also ISO 13485, 7.5.11.

5. (21 CFR 820.120(c)) Labeling shall be stored in a manner that provides proper identification and is designed to prevent mix-ups.[191]

### Distribution[192]

1. (21 CFR 820.160(a))[193] Procedures shall be established for control and distribution of product to ensure the following:
   - That only product approved for release is distributed
   - That purchase orders are reviewed to ensure resolution of ambiguities and errors before product is released for distribution
   - (ISO 13485, 7.2.1 a)) That customer requirements for delivery are met
2. (21 CFR 820.160(a)) Where a product's fitness for use or quality deteriorates over time, procedures shall ensure that expired product or product deteriorated beyond acceptable fitness for use is not distributed.
3. (21 CFR 820.160(b)), (21 CFR 820.65 and Preamble, Section 120)[194] Distribution records shall be maintained that include or refer to the location of the following:
   - (21 CFR 820.160(b)(1)) The name and address of the initial consignee
   - (21 CFR 820.160(b)(2)) The identification and quantity of product shipped
   - (21 CFR 820.160(b)(3)) The date shipped
   - (21 CFR 820.160(b)(4)) Any control number(s) used
4. (21 CFR 820.120(e)) Where a control number is required by regulation because the product is intended for surgical implant or for other reason(s) specified by regulation, that control number shall be on or shall accompany the product through distribution.

---

[191] The same statement is in production section. In this case the duplication is logical because different departments may be using the two different procedures.

[192] A company with products subject to 21 CFR 821 (Medical Device Tracking) will have additional requirements.

[193] See also ISO 13485, 7.5.1.

[194] See also ISO 13485, 7.5.9.2.

## SERVICE AND SUPPORT

### Responsibilities

*Definition of responsibilities in this are dependent upon company organization. To the extent these actions are outsourced, responsibilities should be managed through supplier quality management.*

### Requirements

#### General

1. (21 CFR 820.200(a))[195] For products requiring servicing, instructions and procedures shall be established for performing the servicing and verifying that the servicing meets the specified requirements.
2. (21 CFR 820.200(d))[196] Service reports shall be documented and shall include: (1) The name of the product serviced; (2) Any product identification(s) and control number(s) used; (3) The date of service; (4) The individual(s) servicing the product; (5) The service performed; and (6) The test and inspection data.
3. (21 CFR 820.200(c))[197] Any service report that represents a reportable event shall be documented and addressed as a complaint and shall be processed in accordance with requirements of customer feedback management.
4. (21 CFR 820.200(b) and Preamble, Section 201) Service reports shall be analyzed with appropriate statistical methodology to identify any issues requiring corrective or preventive action. When frequency of servicing is higher than expected the service event should be handled as a complaint.[198]

---

[195] See also ISO 13485, 7.2.1 a), 7.5.4.
[196] See also ISO 13485, 7.5.4.
[197] See also ISO 13485, 7.5.4 for 3 and 4.
[198] Although regulatory statements are not absolutely specific, it is logical, based on the definition of complaint [820.3(b)], to strengthen this statement to require that all unscheduled service events be treated as complaints.

### Installation[199]

1.  (21 CFR 820.170(a))[200] For products requiring installation, adequate installation and inspection instructions shall be established and maintained, including, where appropriate, test procedures. Instructions and procedures shall include directions for ensuring proper installation so that the product will perform as intended after installation.

2.  (21 CFR 820.170(c)) If installation is not carried out by an agent of the company, established procedures shall ensure that the instructions in procedures are distributed with the product or otherwise made available to the person(s) installing the product.

3.  (21 CFR 820.170(b)) If installation is carried out by an agent of the company, procedures shall ensure the following:

    *   That the person installing the product carries out the installation, inspection, and any required testing in accordance with the established instructions and procedures
    *   That the inspection and any test results to demonstrate proper installation are documented

## MARKETING AND SALES[201]

### Responsibilities

*Although clearly this is an area where responsibility for ultimate execution must be with the various business functions, the regulatory and quality departments will need to ensure that the processes are correctly established.*

---

[199] Since products requiring installation by an agent of the company are normally installed by the same staff that provides servicing, this section is included in this Level 2 procedure. A company whose products do not require installation by an agent of the company would logically have no Level 2 procedure for servicing and would include the substance of items 1 and 2 under installation in the Level 2 procedure for handling, storage, preservation, and delivery.

[200] See also ISO 13485, 7.5.3.

[201] Although legal requirements applicable to marketing and sales practices are outside the scope of the QMS, this procedure would also be an appropriate home for enunciating the principles related to those requirements.

## Requirements

### *General*

1. Processes shall be established to ensure that marketing and sales materials are consistent with marketing authorizations.
2. Processes shall be established to ensure that marketing practices worldwide are consistent with legal and regulatory requirements.
3. (ISO 13485, 7.2.1 d)) *Processes shall ensure that needed user training is identified for products to be sold.*
4. (ISO 13485, 7.2.3) Customer communication arrangements shall ensure the following:
   - That product information can be available as needed
   - That customers are aware of mechanisms for enquiries, orders and changes in orders
   - That customers are aware of feedback opportunities, particularly with regard to lodging complaints
5. (ISO 13485, 7.2.2) Order entry processes shall be established in accordance with regulatory requirements to ensure the following:
   - That customers are able to access documented functional and performance information about products prior to purchase
   - That orders are reviewed[202] prior to acceptance to ensure mutual understanding of the requirements and that the orders can be properly filled (including availability of any user training needed)
   - That mechanisms are in place to resolve questions related to changes in orders or misunderstandings
   - That records are maintained of order entry processes

---

# CUSTOMER FEEDBACK MANAGEMENT

## Responsibilities

*A customer service function is usually assigned primary responsibility in this area. The regulatory function should have responsibility to address issues related to potential adverse events. Manufacturing and research and*

---

[202] As noted in the 2003 version of the ISO 13485 standard, there are some circumstances in which a formal review of individual orders may not be possible. In this situation, the applicable review is the review of the catalog, web pages, or advertising materials involved. "ISO 13485:2016, Medical devices: A practical guide" provides guidance regarding website sales.

development should be responsible for investigations related to those areas. Many functions, including marketing and research and development, will have responsibilities related to early warning.

Each employee should have a defined responsibility to ensure that complaints received personally are properly documented.

## Requirements

### General

1. (21 CFR 820.198)[203] Procedures shall be established to ensure the following:
   - (21 CFR 820.198(a)) That complaints[204] are received, reviewed, and evaluated by [a formally designated unit][205]
   - (21 CFR 820.198(a)(1)) That all complaints are processed in a uniform and timely manner
   - (21 CFR 820.198(a)(2)) That oral complaints are documented upon receipt
   - That customer feedback not meeting the definition of complaints shall be addressed in accordance with applicable procedures that address business needs and customer requirements[206]
2. (21 CFR 820.198(a), (e)) Complaint files shall be maintained by [the formally designated complaint unit].[207] The record of the complaint[208] shall include the following:
   - (21 CFR 820.198(a)(1)) The name of the product
   - (21 CFR 820.198(a)(2)) The date the complaint was received
   - (21 CFR 820.198(a)(3)) Any product identification(s) and control number(s) used

---

[203] See also ISO 13485, 7.5.1 f), 8.2.1, 8.2.2.
[204] Companies should note that the definition of "complaint" in ISO 13485 in the new revision is more extensive than the FDA definition. It now includes issues related to services that affect the performance of the product. See ISO 13485:2016, 3.4. Company documentation may need to be brought up to date.
[205] Insert actual name of the group responsible.
[206] Not a regulatory or quality standard requirement but needed for the sake of completeness.
[207] Specify.
[208] Although these records requirements actually apply in the Quality System Regulation to "complaint investigations," in fact prudence dictates that the record be made for each complaint. That is, even in the case for a complaint not resulting in an investigation, this level of detail in the record is advisable.

- (21 CFR 820.198(a)(4)) The name, address, and phone number of the complainant
- (21 CFR 820.198(a)(5)) The nature and details of the complaints
- (21 CFR 820.198(a)(6)) The dates and results of the investigation (unless investigation not required)
- (21 CFR 820.198(a)(7)) Any corrective action taken
- (21 CFR 820.198(a)(8)) Any reply to the complainant

3. (ISO 13485, 8.2.2) If a customer complaint is not followed by corrective and/or preventive action, the reason shall be authorized and recorded.[209]

4. (21 CFR 820.198(f)) When the formally designated complaint unit is located at a site separate from the manufacturing establishment, the investigated complaint(s), and the record(s) of investigation shall be reasonably accessible to the manufacturing establishment.

5. (21 CFR 820.198(g)) If a manufacturer's formally designated complaint unit is located outside of the United States, records of complaints shall be reasonably accessible in the United States at either: (1) A location in the United States where the manufacturer's records are regularly kept; or (2) The location of the initial distributor.

### Investigation

1. (21 CFR 820.198(b)) Each complaint shall be reviewed and evaluated to determine whether an investigation is necessary. If it is determined that an investigation is not necessary, the reason for the decision and the name of the individual responsible for the decision shall be documented.

2. (21 CFR 820.198(c)) Any complaint involving the possible failure of the product, labeling, or packaging to meet any of its specifications[210] shall be reviewed, evaluated, and investigated, unless such investigation has already been performed for a similar complaint and another investigation is not necessary.

---

[209] One possible reason may be data showing that the issue does not meet CAPA criteria (in which case a correction must be carried out).

[210] Note that this wording (from the FDA) means that if there is an inconvenience issue associated with a product and the company has decided to take no action concerning this issue and has documented this decision, this can be an acceptable reason not to conduct an investigation.

3. (21 CFR 820.100(a)(6)[211] If investigation indicates activities outside the company were a factor in relation to the issue, information shall be disseminated to those responsible.

## Event Reporting

1. (21 CFR 820.198(a)(3) and (ISO 13485, 8.2.3) Each complaint shall be evaluated to determine whether it represents an event that is required to be reported to FDA under Medical Device Reporting and/or to other regulatory authorities worldwide under Vigilance Reporting.
2. (21 CFR 820.198(d))[212] Any complaint that represents an event which must be reported to any regulatory authority shall be promptly reviewed, evaluated, and investigated by designated individual(s) in order to meet reporting deadlines.[213]
3. (21 CFR 820.198(d)) Records for reportable and potentially reportable events shall be maintained in a separate portion of the complaint files or otherwise clearly identified. In addition to the information required above for complaint records, records of investigation related to reportable events shall include a determination of the following:
   - (21 CFR 820.198(d)(1)) Whether the product failed to meet specifications
   - (21 CFR 820.198(d)(2)) Whether the product was being used for treatment or diagnosis
   - (21 CFR 820.198(d)(3)) The relationship, if any, of the product to the reported incident or adverse event

## Postmarket Surveillance

1. (MDR, Art. 83; IVDR, Art. 78)[214] For each product, a postmarket surveillance system shall be established that is proportionate to the risk for the product. Procedures shall specify required plans and reports.

---

[211] See also ISO 13485, 8.2.2.
[212] See also ISO 13485, 8.2.3.
[213] A table specifying reporting deadlines in applicable markets for various types of adverse events should be included.
[214] See also ISO 13485, 8.5.1.

2. (ISO 13485, 8.2.1) Procedures shall be established to provide early warning of quality problems. In addition to the system for customer feedback management, the early warning system includes the following:
   - Customer/user surveys
   - Regulatory authority communications
   - Regulatory authority compliance-related communications
   - Peer-reviewed journals and trade journals
   - Website postings and social media

   Feedback shall be used as possible input to product risk management files, as well as for product or process improvement.

3. (21 CFR 820.100) and (ISO 13485, 8.2.1) Where identified quality problems meet criteria specified for corrective or preventive action, such action, including issue and implementation of advisory notices if appropriate,[215] shall be initiated according to applicable procedures.

4. (MDD, Annex X, 1.1c; MDR, Annex XIV, Part B; IVDR, Annex XIII, Part B)[216] Postmarket clinical studies/performance evaluation and/or other postproduction experience reviews shall be conducted where required.[217]

# CORRECTIVE AND PREVENTIVE ACTION

## Responsibilities

*Although the quality function should have primary responsibility in this area, all departments should be assigned responsibility to follow through with actions as needed to ensure a fully effective CAPA system.*

*For Field Corrective Actions, the regulatory function should have primary responsibility.*

---

[215] Registrars/notified nodies expect to find explicit reference to the concept of "advisory notices."

[216] See also ISO 13485, 8.2.1.

[217] Council Directive 93/42/EEC of 14 June 1993 concerning medical devices as last amended by Directive 2007/47/EC of the European Parliament and of the Council of 5 September 2007 and Council Directive 90/385/EEC of 20 June 1990 on the approximation of the laws of the Member States relating to active implantable medical devices last amended by Directive 2007/47/EC of the European Parliament and of the Council of 5 September 2007. In addition, FDA may require postapproval studies as a condition for PreMarket Approval (PMA) or may require manufacturers of certain Class II or Class III devices to conduct postmarket surveillance studies. Other authorities may have similar requirements.

# Requirements

## *General*

1. (21 CFR 820.100(a))[218] A Corrective and Preventive Action System shall be established to eliminate causes of nonconformities and potential nonconformities and to fulfill quality and regulatory requirements.
2. (21 CFR 820.100(a)(1)) The CAPA System shall provide for appropriate statistical analysis of processes, work operations, concessions, quality audit reports, quality records, service records, complaints, returned product, post market surveillance and other sources of quality data to identify existing and potential causes of nonconformities relating to product, processes or the QMS.
3. The CAPA System should provide the possibility for any employee to bring concerns to the attention of management for possible corrective or preventive action.[219]
4. (21 CFA 820.100 and Preamble, Section 159) The CAPA System shall incorporate criteria based on patient/user risk for determination of those issues that must be addressed by corrective or preventive action and those issues that may be addressed by a correction.
5. (21 CFA 820.100 and Preamble, Section 159) For issues that must be addressed by corrective or preventive action, the system shall provide for the following:
   - (21 CFR 820.100(a)(2)) Investigating the cause of nonconformities related to products, processes and the QMS
   - (21 CFR 820.100(a)(3)) Identifying the action(s) needed to correct and prevent recurrence, including where necessary the updating of documentation
   - (ISO 13485, 8.5.2) *Ensuring that actions needed are taken without undue delay*
   - (21 CFA 820.100 and Preamble, Section 159) Ensuring that actions taken are appropriate to the effect of the nonconformities
   - (21 CFR 820.100(a)(4)) Verifying or validating the corrective and preventive action to ensure that such action is effective and does not adversely affect products, processes, or the QMS

---

[218] See also ISO 13485, 8.5.2, 8.5.3 for 1, 2, and 5.
[219] Not explicitly required by regulation or standards.

- (21 CFR 820.100(a)(5)) Implementing and recording changes in methods and procedures needed to correct and prevent identified quality problems
- (21 CFR 820.100(a)(6)) Ensuring that information related to quality problems or nonconforming product is disseminated to responsible parties

6. (21 CFR 820.100(a)(7)) Relevant information shall be submitted for management review, such as:
   - Identified quality problems and resulting corrective and preventive actions
   - The functioning of the CAPA System itself[220]

7. (21 CFR 820.100(b)) Ensure documentation of the provisions of this procedure. CAPA documentation shall not include reports of internal audits or supplier audits.[221]

### Field Corrective Actions, Including FDA Corrections,[222] and Removals

1. (21 CFR 7; 21 CFR 806; ISO 13485, 7.2.3 d), 8.3.3) Procedures shall be established for carrying out field corrective actions in accordance with applicable regulations and standards. These procedures, capable of implementation at any time, shall include provision for advisory notices[223]/field safety notices.

2. Procedures should ensure that product issues judged to be covered by both 21 CFR 806.10 and 21 CFR 806.20 are reported to the FDA.[224]

---

[220] Not an explicit requirement of regulation or standards.

[221] CAPA records may be inspected by the FDA whereas FDA policy dictates that audit reports should not be inspected. Therefore, it is important to ensure that these reports are not incorporated into the CAPA documentation even if the audit report was what led to the CAPA. Nevertheless, there should be a single CAPA system; it is not appropriate to keep CAPAs derived from internal audits in a completely separate system.

[222] The FDA use of the term "correction" is in relation to correction of product problems in the field and is usually one component of a larger corrective action. Because this FDA usage can become confused with the more standard usage (where the term applies to simply fixing a nonconformity) it is useful to use the term "FDA correction" when addressing that specific subject.

[223] As noted earlier, registrars/notified bodies expect to find explicit reference to the term "advisory notice."

[224] This is the recommended practice for the following reasons. First, the ultimate authority as to whether an issue falls under 806.10 or 806.20 is the FDA. When the FDA arrives for an inspection, they will review all the items covered under 806. If they disagree with the original assessment, this will create problems for the company. Furthermore, after the inspection visit, all the items not reported under 806.20 will become listed on the FDA website. This can confuse customers, who may think this is a new recall, rather than the one they were already notified of. Thus, for sound business reasons, it is usually best to report all 806 items, no matter which category is judged to apply. (Gina Brackett, FDA Compliance Officer, Cincinnati District Office, personal communication).

# CONTROL OF NONCONFORMING PRODUCT

## Responsibilities

*The manufacturing and quality functions normally have primary responsibilities in this area.*

*Employees should have a defined responsibility to report any observed non-conforming product in a manner that allows proper addressing of the nonconformity.*

## Requirements

### General

1. (21 CFR 820.90(a))[225] Procedures shall be established to control product that does not conform to specified requirements and to prevent its unintended use or delivery. These procedures shall address the following:
   - Identification
   - Documentation
   - Evaluation
   - Segregation
   - Disposition
2. (21 CFR 820.90(a)) Evaluation of the nonconformance shall include:
   - The determination of the need for an investigation[226]
   - Notification of the persons or organizations responsible for the nonconformance.
3. (21 CFR 820.90(a)) The evaluation and any investigation shall be documented.

### Review and Disposition

1. (21 CFR 820.90(b)(1)) Procedures for review and disposition of nonconforming product shall be established that address the following:
   - Responsibility for review
   - Authority for disposition
   - The review and disposition process

---

[225] See also ISO 13485, 8.3.

[226] Related Level 3 procedures should indicate criteria for these determinations.

2. (21 CFR 820.90(b)(1)) Three options shall be possible for disposition of nonconforming product detected prior to use or delivery, including:

   - Taking action to eliminate the detected nonconformity
   - Taking action to preclude the original intended use or application
   - Authorizing its use, release or acceptance under concession (((ISO 13485, 8.3.2) only if regulatory requirements are met).[227]

3. (21 CFR 820.90(b)(1) and Preamble, Section 156)[228] Disposition of nonconforming product shall be documented. Documentation shall include the scientific justification for use of nonconforming product under concession and the signature of the individual(s) authorizing the use.

4. (21 CFR 820.90(b)(2) and Preamble, Section 157)[229] Procedures shall be established for rework that meet the following requirements:

   - Retesting and reevaluation of the nonconforming product after rework to ensure the product meets current approved specifications.
   - (ISO 13485, 8.3.4) Rework instructions with the same authorization and approval as the original work instruction.
   - Prior to authorization of the work instruction, a documented determination of potential adverse effect of the rework upon product.

5. (21 CFR 820.90(b)(2)) Rework and reevaluation activities, including a determination of any adverse effect from the rework upon the product, shall be documented in the Device History Record.

6. (21 CFR 806, 21 CFR 820.100)[230] When nonconforming product is detected after delivery or use, action shall be taken that is appropriate to the effects or potential effects of the nonconformity (see Customer Feedback Management process).

---

[227] Some companies prefer not to permit the third option. However, since there is the possibility of an issue's being entirely cosmetic, such as a part with not the exactly specified color, it may be prudent to allow the option provided sufficient investigation has been conducted to ensure that the issue is indeed merely cosmetic.

[228] See also ISO 13485, 8.3.2 for 3 and 6.

[229] See also ISO 13485, 8.3.4.

[230] See also ISO 13485, 8.3.3.

# Appendix D: Example Level 3 Flowchart Procedure

## COMMENT

The primary intent of Appendix D is to provide an example of a flowchart procedure. This type of procedure is particularly useful for Level 3, where the intent is to describe the detailed steps for how a particular subject must be addressed. Some comments about the structure of the appendix are in order:

1. As in the case in Appendix C, this example is not intended to be a complete procedure. A complete procedure will have additional sections, such as purpose, scope, references, document history, and other sections as required.
2. The flowchart precedes the text of the detailed steps. A visual picture of the required steps is valuable for users to provide a clear impression quickly of what they are expected to do. Flowcharts are often treated as an optional attachment to a procedure when they can be more effective as the heart of the procedure. The flowchart flows clearly from top to bottom; flowcharts that loop back in awkward ways cause the reader's eyes to glaze over.
3. The table following the flowchart adds the details that do not readily fit on a flowchart. It is critical that the table entries have a one-to-one correspondence with the numbering on the flowchart.
4. The table functions essentially like a playscript style of procedure (see Appendix E). In fact, if the two columns were reversed and the flowchart omitted, this would be a playscript procedure. For some reason, although playscript procedures can be useful in making clear who is responsible to do what and in what order, there seems to be a resistance to playscript procedures on the part of many users.

However, when the same information is presented as a table with a one-to-one correspondence to a flowchart, there is a much readier acceptance of the approach.

Because this example also addresses a critical subject for any business, some comments regarding the subject matter are appropriate.

1. Rather than identifying the subject as complaint management, it is useful to use a more generic term, such as "customer feedback management." This draws attention to the fact that these contacts may involve concerns that go beyond regulatory definitions of "complaint," to include categories such as inquiries and what we may call "business issues." A "business issue" would be a customer concern about a late delivery or an incorrect delivery. A business issue is definitely a complaint in the everyday sense of the word, but does not require the same level of attention as does a complaint in the regulatory sense. It is useful to maintain the distinction. This does not mean that business issues should be handled in a careless manner; a business issue can lose a customer just as fast as a regulatory complaint.

2. In preparing the example, an assumption has been made that this procedure applies to a moderate-sized company, with local organizations in multiple countries. For sake of simplicity in the example, we assume also that complaints are passed to the headquarters location of the company in the United States for assessment and investigation, and that a single electronic documentation system for management of customer contacts makes worldwide information available at the headquarters location. (In any case, there must be in place a system for ensuring that information about regulatory complaints is available at a headquarters location.)

3. Because of the assumption that there is a call center in each country, it is also assumed that individuals at the call centers will have either a more-detailed local procedure (certainly necessary in the case of language differences) or sufficient guidance from within the software application to ensure that issues (particularly reportability issues) are appropriately handled.

4. In the initial steps of this procedure, the exact order is normally not critical, since these steps will all be carried out within a very short time frame.

5. As action proceeds on the complaint, it is critical that the responsible parties communicate on the various aspects that may be involved: assessment, reportability, sample receipt and testing, corrective action, other investigation, communication to the customer, and ensuring that documentation is complete. The larger the company, the more difficult the communication, and large companies may need to extend the flowchart and the detailed instruction to ensure that responsible parties are informed of all actions. A good software application can be indispensable for ensuring the efficiency of such communication, and can drive or facilitate the workflow described in the flowchart.

# LEVEL 3 CUSTOMER FEEDBACK MANAGEMENT

## Procedure

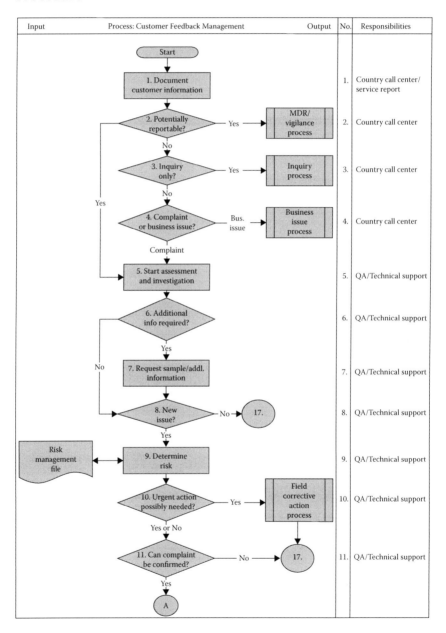

**FIGURE D.1**
Flowchart for customer feedback management, Part 1.

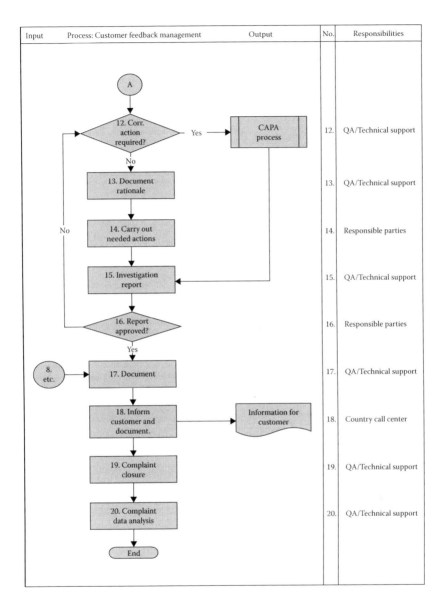

**FIGURE D.2**
Flowchart for customer feedback management, Part 2.

| Action (See Figure D.1) | Responsibility |
| --- | --- |
| 1. Upon receiving a call, document customer information specified; collect information that may be important to an investigation.[1] Request sample product where appropriate. Service calls meeting the definition of complaint must be documented in the same manner as complaints.[2] <br>Note: Local procedures must ensure that all employees are aware of the responsibility to ensure that complaints communicated to them must be documented in a timely manner.[3] | Country call center/Service report |
| 2. If the information suggests that the complaint may involve a reportable issue, forward the documented information in accordance with the procedure(s) for addressing medical device reporting/vigilance.[4] Maintain the record as a complaint but ensure that it is identified as potentially reportable. | Country call center |
| 3. If the information indicates that the customer is simply making an inquiry, forward the inquiry in accordance with the procedures for inquiries.[5] Do not maintain as a complaint. | Country call center |
| 4. If the information indicates that this is a business issue rather than a complaint, forward the issue in accordance with the procedures for business issues. If the issue is a complaint, forward the issue to the responsible department.[6] | Country call center |
| 5. Continue assessment of the complaint. | Quality Assurance/ Technical Support |

*(Continued)*

[1] The customer information may be specified in the software application or on a paper form. This information may be different, depending upon whether the customer concern is an inquiry, a business issue, or a regulatory complaint. The information that must be specified for regulatory complaints is identified in applicable regulations.

In some cases, particularly for self-test products, it may be possible to carry out a full investigation by means of the initial telephone contact. If the problem is a use error, the call center representative may be able to identify and correct the problem on the telephone. Such calls must still be logged as complaints, because subsequent analysis of the frequency of use errors may indicate an issue that requires corrective action.

[2] This does not mean that the same software application or the same form must be used.

[3] This is particularly important with regard to sales and marketing staff, but also includes, for example, research and development representatives communicating with customers.

[4] Each company doing business in countries outside its home country must find an appropriate balance between the central organization's need to ensure consistent handling of issues worldwide (within the limitation of insufficiently harmonized regulations on the subject) and each country organization's need to comply with the laws and regulations of that country. The bottom line is that if a country organization believes an issue must be reported, they will choose to obey their interpretation of their law rather than fulfill a procedural requirement from the central organization of their company. Working with country organizations before any incident occurs can make this kind of breakdown extremely rare.

[5] If there is no established procedure for inquiries, this instruction will simply state to forward the question to the appropriate department.

[6] Each company must determine the appropriate group(s) for addressing complaints; this is often quality assurance or technical support (as indicated here) but need not be. The nature of the product may determine the specific group to which the complaint is assigned.

| Action (See Figures D.1 and D.2) | Responsibility |
| --- | --- |
| 6. Determine if additional information is needed or if sample product was not requested but should have been requested. If Yes, go to step 7. If No, go directly to step 8. | Quality Assurance/ Technical Support |
| 7. Request additional information or sample product. Ensure that such requests are followed up at least two times in cases where the information or sample are not forthcoming. | Quality Assurance/ Technical Support |
| 8. Determine if this is a new issue. If No, go to step 17. If Yes, go to step 9. | Quality Assurance/ Technical Support |
| 9. Using information in the risk management file,[7] determine the risks involved with the situation.<br>Note: The flowchart shows a two-headed arrow to indicate that a revision of the risk management file (RMF) is required if the complaint represents a risk not previously identified. | Quality Assurance/ Technical Support |
| 10. Decide if urgent field action may be needed based on available information. If Yes, process according to the procedures for field corrective action.[8] Ensure documentation for the field corrective action is connected with the complaint documentation; go to step 17. Whether Yes or No, proceed to step 11. | Quality Assurance/ Technical Support |
| 11. Determine whether the complaint can be confirmed. (If customer sample is not available, consider whether a retained sample should be tested.) If Yes (complaint is confirmed), go to step 12. If No, document and proceed to step 17.<br>Note: Inability to confirm does not mean that the customer has imagined what was reported. Consider possible scientific explanations for the discrepancy, and consider also whether further investigation may be appropriate even with the lack of confirmation. | Quality Assurance/ Technical Support |
| 12. Determine whether the complaint fulfills the criteria requiring corrective action. If Yes, process according to the procedure(s) for corrective and preventive action. If No, go to step 13.<br>Note: The CAPA process may ultimately lead also to the field corrective action process. | Quality Assurance/ Technical Support |

(*Continued*)

---

[7] This is one of many reasons why the risk management file, or at least key components of it, should be maintained and available electronically in order to be easily searchable.

[8] Here we assume that the field corrective action process involves at least three elements: (1) a decision on a stop ship notice to prevent product from leaving company control; (2) a decision on whether a corrective action in the field is required; and (3) the details of how a field corrective action must be executed. At this point in the workflow of this procedure, placing a stop ship hold on potentially affected product would not be unusual.

| Action (See Figure D.2) | Responsibility |
|---|---|
| 13. Document the rationale for not carrying out a corrective action. | Quality Assurance/ Technical Support |
| 14. Carry out needed corrections and any other appropriate actions. | Quality Assurance/ Technical Support |
| 15. Complete the investigation report.[9] If a corrective action was carried out, the investigation report should include or reference the CAPA documentation. | Quality Assurance/ Technical Support |
| 16. Can the report be approved? If No, go to step 12. If Yes, go to step 17. | Responsible parties[10] |
| 17. Complete the documentation for the complaint. | Quality Assurance/ Technical Support |
| 18. Communicate information to the customer and document the communication. | Country Call Center |
| 19. Close complaint. | Quality Assurance/ Technical Support |
| 20. Analyze complaints for possible corrective or preventive action.[11] | Quality Assurance/ Technical Support |

---

[9] Some companies specify a procedure for investigations. In such cases, a reference to the investigation procedure would need to be integrated into this process.

[10] Each company must determine the appropriate manager(s) to approve the report.

[11] This action may require further elaboration, either in a separate procedure or as an extension of this procedure.

# Appendix E: Example Level 3 Playscript Procedure

## COMMENT

Playscript procedures contain all the usual sections of a procedure, such as purpose, scope, definitions, references, records, etc. However, there is no need for a separate responsibility section, since the structure of the procedure section itself makes this unnecessary.

See Appendix D for comments and footnotes about the subject of customer feedback management.

## LEVEL 3 CUSTOMER FEEDBACK MANAGEMENT

### Procedure

| Responsibility | Action |
|---|---|
| Country call center/Service report | 1. Upon receiving a call, document customer information specified; collect information that may be important to an investigation. Request sample product where appropriate. Service calls meeting the definition of complaint must be documented in the same manner as complaints. |
| Country call center | 2. If the information suggests that the complaint may involve a reportable issue, forward the documented information in accordance with the procedures for addressing medical device reporting/vigilance. Maintain the record as a complaint but ensure that it is identified as potentially reportable. |
| Country call center | 3. If the information indicates that the customer is simply making an inquiry, forward the inquiry in accordance with the procedures for inquiries. Do not maintain as a complaint. |

*(Continued)*

| Responsibility | Action |
|---|---|
| Country call center | 4. If the information indicates that this is a business issue rather than a complaint, forward the issue in accordance with the procedures for business issues. If the issue is a complaint, forward the issue to [the responsible department].[1] |
| QA/Technical Support | 5. Continue assessment of the complaint. |
| QA/Technical Support | 6. Determine if additional information is needed or if sample product was not requested but should have been requested. If Yes, go to step 7. If No, go directly to step 8. |
| QA/Technical Support | 7. Request additional information or sample product. Ensure that such requests are followed up at least two times in cases where the information or sample are not forthcoming. |
| QA/Technical Support | 8. Determine if this is a new issue. If No, go to step 17. If Yes, go to step 9. |
| QA/Technical Support | 9. Using information in the risk management file (RMF), determine the risks involved with the situation. Note: A revision of the RMF is required if the complaint represents a risk not previously identified. |
| QA/Technical Support | 10. Decide if urgent field action may be needed based on available information. If Yes, process according to the procedures for field corrective action. Ensure documentation for the field corrective action is connected with the complaint documentation; go to step 17. Whether Yes or No, proceed to step 11. |
| QA/Technical Support | 11. Determine whether the complaint can be confirmed. (If customer sample is not available, consider whether a retained sample should be tested.) If Yes (complaint is confirmed), go to step 12. If No, document and proceed to step 17. Note: Inability to confirm does not mean that the customer has imagined what was reported. Consider possible scientific explanations for the discrepancy, and consider also whether further investigation may be appropriate even with the lack of confirmation. |
| QA/Technical Support | 12. Determine whether the complaint fulfills the criteria requiring corrective action. If Yes, process according to the procedures for corrective and preventive action. If No, go to step 13. |
| QA/Technical Support | 13. Document the rationale for not carrying out a corrective action. |
| QA/Technical Support | 14. Carry out needed corrections and any other appropriate actions. |

*(Continued)*

[1] Assumed for this example to be quality assurance or technical support.

| Responsibility | Action |
|---|---|
| QA/Technical Support | 15. Complete the investigation report. If a corrective action was carried out, the investigation report should include or reference the CAPA documentation. |
| Responsible parties | 16. Can the report be approved? If No, go to step 12. If Yes, go to step 17. |
| QA/Technical Support | 17. Complete the documentation for the complaint. |
| Country Call Center | 18. Communicate information to the customer and document the communication. |
| QA/Technical Support | 19. Close complaint. |
| QA/Technical Support | 20. Analyze complaints for possible corrective or preventive action. |

# Index

Printed in the United States
by Baker & Taylor Publisher Services